50 Founder & Builder Stories

DANIEL BOYD

DEDICATION

To the fearless dreamers, relentless builders, and visionary entrepreneurs who shape our world through their unwavering dedication and transformative ideas.

To the mentors, advisors, and supporters who provided guidance, wisdom, and invaluable resources along the way. Your belief in this book made it possible.

This book is dedicated to the remarkable individuals who dared to challenge the status quo, defy limits, and build something extraordinary. Your stories are an inspiration to all those who believe in the power of ideas, the pursuit of dreams, and the relentless pursuit of progress.

Thank you to the founders, builders, and visionaries who have forever changed our world. Your stories deserve to be shared, celebrated, and passed on to inspire the next generation of innovators and builders.

With deepest appreciation,
Daniel

Table of Contents

0. Introduction

In the vast landscape of entrepreneurship, there exist extraordinary individuals whose relentless ambition, audacious ideas, and unwavering determination have left an indelible mark on our world. They are the visionaries, the trailblazers who dared to challenge the status quo and redefine the possibilities. Their stories are the essence of inspiration, the fuel that ignites the entrepreneurial spirit within us.

Welcome to "50 Founder & Builder Stories" Within these pages, we embark on a remarkable journey that unveils the extraordinary lives and ventures of fifty exceptional individuals who forever transformed industries, societies, and the way we perceive the world.

These founders, armed with nothing but their unyielding passion and insatiable curiosity, have disrupted conventional norms, launching ventures that defied expectations and redefined the very fabric of our existence. From the realms of technology to retail, from finance to entertainment, they have revolutionized the way we communicate, learn, work, and live. Each chapter in this book unveils a remarkable tale of triumph over adversity, of resilience in the face of challenges, and of groundbreaking innovation that has shaped our modern landscape.

Discover the legendary path of Elon Musk, whose ventures have extended our reach beyond Earth's limits with Tesla's electric vehicles and SpaceX's awe-inspiring missions to space. Dive into the revolutionary vision of Jeff Bezos, who transformed online commerce forever with the creation of Amazon. Witness the social connectivity revolution ignited by Mark Zuckerberg through the inception of Facebook, a platform that has reshaped the way we connect and share our lives.

But this book goes beyond the well-known names. It delves deep into the stories of lesser-known pioneers who have forged their own path, leaving a profound impact on their respective industries. Uncover the journey of Payal Kadakia, the relentless force behind ClassPass, empowering individuals to experience a wide range of fitness classes. Explore the vision of Anne Wojcicki, whose company, 23andMe, has revolutionized personalized genomics, empowering individuals to gain insight into their genetic makeup.

As you immerse yourself in the tales of these remarkable founders, you will witness the trials and tribulations they faced on their entrepreneurial odyssey. From the euphoria of early successes to the depths of uncertainty and the resilience required to rise above failure, their stories epitomize the roller coaster journey of entrepreneurship.

"Trailblazers: Pioneering Founders Who Shaped the Future" is a tribute to these extraordinary men and women who defied conventions, shattered boundaries, and transformed our world. It is an exploration of their unwavering passion, relentless pursuit of their dreams, and their profound impact on society. Their stories will inspire you to embrace your own audacious ideas, challenge the status quo, and leave an enduring legacy of your own.

So, join us on this exhilarating expedition into the lives of those who dared to dream big, dared to disrupt, and dared to shape the future. Let their stories ignite the fire within you and set you on a path to creating your own indelible mark in the world of entrepreneurship.

1. Elon Musk

Elon Musk: a name that has become synonymous with audacity, ambition, and groundbreaking innovation. From the early days of his entrepreneurial journey to becoming one of the most influential figures of the 21st century, Elon Musk has consistently pushed the boundaries of what is deemed possible. His relentless drive to revolutionize industries and tackle humanity's most pressing challenges has made him a true trailblazer in the world of entrepreneurship.

Born in Pretoria, South Africa, in 1971, Musk's journey began with an insatiable curiosity and an insuppressible desire to explore the realms of science and technology. Even as a young child, he displayed an exceptional intellect and an ability to think beyond the confines of conventional wisdom. It was this unquenchable thirst for knowledge that would later fuel his ambitious ventures.

Musk's entrepreneurial journey took off in the late 1990s when he co-founded Zip2, a software company that provided business directories and maps for newspapers. This endeavor laid the foundation for his future successes, showcasing his ability to identify gaps in the market and create innovative solutions. In 1999, Compaq acquired Zip2, yielding Musk his first taste of entrepreneurial triumph.

Undeterred by this initial success, Musk set his sights even higher. In 2002, he co-founded SpaceX (Space Exploration Technologies Corp.) with the audacious goal of revolutionizing space travel and making humanity a multi-planetary species. With SpaceX, Musk aimed to tackle the formidable challenges that had hindered progress in space exploration for decades. His relentless pursuit of innovation and cost-efficiency drove SpaceX to develop groundbreaking technologies, including the world's first privately funded liquid-fueled rocket to reach orbit, the Falcon 1, and the renowned Falcon 9 rocket that revolutionized the space launch industry.

While SpaceX propelled Musk into the public eye, it was his involvement with Tesla, the electric vehicle company, that truly reshaped the transportation industry. In 2004, Musk joined Tesla as Chairman and eventually became its CEO, leading the charge towards sustainable transportation. With Tesla, Musk dared to challenge the dominance of gasoline-powered vehicles, defying skeptics who doubted the viability of electric cars. Through relentless research and development, Tesla introduced high-performance electric vehicles that shattered preconceived notions about electric mobility. The Model S, Model 3, Model X, and Model Y have since become icons of cutting-edge design and technological innovation, pushing the automotive industry towards a greener future.

Beyond space travel and electric vehicles, Musk's vision expanded further with his involvement in other ventures. His interest in renewable energy led to the creation of SolarCity, a solar energy services company that aimed to accelerate the world's transition to sustainable power. Additionally, Musk's fascination with the potential of artificial intelligence (AI) led him to co-found Neuralink, a neurotechnology company focused on developing brain-computer interfaces to enhance human capabilities.

Elon Musk's relentless pursuit of ambitious projects has not been without challenges and setbacks. From production delays to technical hurdles, he has faced numerous obstacles along the way. However, it is Musk's unwavering determination and ability to rally his teams that have propelled his ventures forward, defying expectations and driving change on a global scale.

Musk's influence extends beyond the realms of technology and business. His bold vision has inspired countless individuals to dream bigger and think outside the box. He has become a cultural icon, revered for his unrelenting pursuit of innovation, his boldness in challenging established industries, and his commitment to pushing humanity towards a more sustainable and interplanetary future.

As we delve deeper into Elon Musk's journey, we will witness the triumphs, the setbacks, and the sheer audacity that has made him a transformative force. His story serves as a powerful reminder that, with passion, resilience, and a willingness to challenge the status quo, remarkable achievements are within our grasp. Elon Musk's relentless pursuit of innovation is a testament to the incredible potential of human imagination and the profound impact one individual can have on shaping the future of our world.

2. Jeff Bezos

A name that is instantly associated with unrelenting innovation, disruptive entrepreneurship, and the complete upheaval of the retail industry is that of Jeff Bezos. From humble beginnings to becoming one of the wealthiest individuals on the planet, Bezos's visionary leadership has redefined industries and reshaped the way we shop, communicate, and live. His remarkable journey is a testament to the power of audacious ideas, unwavering determination, and a deep understanding of the ever-evolving needs of consumers.

Born in Albuquerque, New Mexico, in 1964, Bezos displayed an early penchant for exploration and intellectual curiosity. After graduating from Princeton University with degrees in electrical engineering and computer science, he embarked on a path that would forever change the face of commerce. In 1994, Bezos founded Amazon, an online bookstore that would soon grow to become the e-commerce behemoth we know today.

Bezos's audacity was evident from the outset. In an era when the internet was still in its nascent stages, he recognized the untapped potential of online retail and seized the opportunity to disrupt traditional brick-and-mortar stores. With an unwavering belief in the power of technology, Bezos envisioned a future where customers could effortlessly browse and purchase a vast array of products from the comfort of their own homes.

Under Bezos's leadership, Amazon rapidly expanded its product offerings, diversifying into various categories beyond books. From electronics to apparel, from household goods to streaming services, Amazon evolved into an all-encompassing marketplace, driven by Bezos's customer-centric philosophy. He understood that convenience, selection, and competitive pricing were paramount to creating a seamless shopping experience, and he relentlessly pursued these goals.

One of Bezos's most groundbreaking innovations was the introduction of Amazon Prime in 2005. With Prime, he redefined the concept of customer loyalty and satisfaction by offering expedited shipping and a host of additional benefits, such as access to streaming content through Amazon Prime Video. This move not only solidified Amazon's position as a dominant force in e-commerce but also transformed consumer expectations for convenience and immediacy.

Bezos's visionary thinking extended beyond retail. In 2000, he founded Blue Origin, a private aerospace company with the audacious goal of making space travel more accessible. By investing in reusable rocket technology and pushing the boundaries of space exploration, Bezos aimed to foster a future where humanity could colonize other planets and expand our understanding of the cosmos.

Throughout his journey, Bezos faced his fair share of challenges and skepticism. From navigating the dot-com bubble to weathering criticism from competitors and industry experts, he remained steadfast in his pursuit of long-term growth and innovation. Bezos's leadership style, characterized by calculated risk-taking, relentless experimentation, and a focus on long-term vision, set Amazon apart as a company willing to disrupt itself to stay ahead of the curve.

Beyond Amazon and Blue Origin, Bezos's influence extended to other ventures, such as his ownership of The Washington Post, a renowned newspaper at the forefront of digital journalism. Additionally, in 2021, Bezos stepped down as CEO of Amazon to focus on philanthropy, environmental initiatives, and his passion for space exploration.

Jeff Bezos's entrepreneurial journey is a testament to the transformative power of innovation and the ability to envision a future that others may deem impossible. His relentless pursuit of customer satisfaction, his unwavering commitment to long-term growth, and his boldness in embracing emerging technologies have left an indelible mark on the world of e-commerce and beyond.

As we explore the remarkable story of Jeff Bezos, we will witness the triumphs, the setbacks, and the unwavering vision that propelled him from an online bookstore to a global empire. His journey serves as an inspiration to aspiring entrepreneurs, demonstrating that with relentless ambition, unwavering commitment, and a profound understanding of consumer needs, one can reshape industries, redefine customer experiences, and leave an enduring legacy that extends far beyond the realm of business.

3. Mark Zuckerberg

The word "social media revolution" is practically inseparable from the name Mark Zuckerberg at this point. From his college dorm room to the global stage, Zuckerberg's entrepreneurial journey has been marked by groundbreaking innovation, cultural impact, and navigating the complexities of privacy and connectivity. His relentless pursuit of connecting people and building communities has reshaped the way we interact, communicate, and share our lives.

Born in 1984 in White Plains, New York, Zuckerberg displayed a prodigious talent for programming and a keen interest in technology from an early age. While studying at Harvard University, he launched "The Facebook" in 2004, a social networking platform initially limited to Harvard students. The platform quickly gained popularity, expanding to other universities and eventually opening its doors to the public as Facebook.

Zuckerberg's vision went beyond creating a simple social networking site. He aimed to build a global community that transcended geographical boundaries, allowing individuals to connect, share, and engage with one another effortlessly. The exponential growth of Facebook, fueled by its user-friendly interface and innovative features, quickly propelled it to the forefront of the digital landscape.

Under Zuckerberg's leadership, Facebook revolutionized the way people communicate and share information. Features like the News Feed, introduced in 2006, transformed the platform into a personalized hub of updates, news, and shared content. Zuckerberg's commitment to constant iteration and improvement led to the introduction of features like photo tagging, events, and groups, further enhancing the social experience and solidifying Facebook's dominance.

Zuckerberg's entrepreneurial journey has not been without challenges. Privacy concerns, data breaches, and allegations of improper use of user data have tested his leadership and forced Facebook to confront critical issues head-on. However, Zuckerberg's response to these challenges has been characterized by a commitment to transparency, privacy reforms, and efforts to foster a safer and more secure online environment.

Beyond Facebook, Zuckerberg's ambitions have extended to various other ventures. In 2012, he spearheaded the acquisition of Instagram, recognizing the immense potential of the photo-sharing platform. This move solidified Facebook's presence in the mobile space and expanded its reach among younger demographics. Subsequently, in 2014, Facebook acquired WhatsApp, a messaging platform with a global user base, further broadening its portfolio of social communication tools.

Zuckerberg's influence reaches beyond the realm of social media. In 2015, he and his wife Priscilla Chan launched the Chan Zuckerberg Initiative, a philanthropic organization focused on addressing challenges in areas such as education, health, and scientific research. This venture reflects Zuckerberg's commitment to utilizing his resources and influence to drive positive societal change and make a lasting impact on a global scale.

As we delve deeper into Mark Zuckerberg's journey, we witness the triumphs, controversies, and evolution of Facebook. His relentless pursuit of connecting the world and his unwavering belief in the power of technology to foster meaningful connections have made him a cultural icon and a symbol of the digital age.

Mark Zuckerberg's entrepreneurial path serves as a powerful reminder that innovation can reshape entire industries and redefine how we interact. While facing complex challenges, he continues to navigate the ever-changing landscape of technology, seeking to balance the pursuit of growth with the responsibility of safeguarding user trust and privacy.

Through his vision and the platform he created, Zuckerberg has empowered billions of individuals to connect, share ideas, and build communities. His impact on the world of social media and his commitment to making a positive difference exemplify the potential of entrepreneurship to drive transformative change in society.

As we embark on the journey of Mark Zuckerberg, we unravel the story of a visionary who dared to reimagine human connection in the digital age and left an indelible mark on the way we connect and engage with one another.

4. Larry Page

Larry Page: an innovator, a technologist, and a visionary whose relentless pursuit of organizing and making information accessible has transformed the way we navigate the digital world. From co-founding Google to revolutionizing online search and beyond, Page's entrepreneurial journey has been marked by an unwavering commitment to innovation, a thirst for knowledge, and a profound impact on the way we access and interact with information.

Born in East Lansing, Michigan, in 1973, Page exhibited a deep passion for technology from an early age. He graduated from Stanford University with a Bachelor of Science degree in computer engineering, where he met his future business partner, Sergey Brin. Together, Page and Brin embarked on a journey that would reshape the internet landscape forever.

In 1998, Page and Brin co-founded Google, initially as a research project aimed at organizing the vast amount of information available on the internet. Their groundbreaking algorithm, PageRank, revolutionized online search by ranking web pages based on their relevance and popularity. This innovative approach to search engine technology propelled Google to unprecedented levels of accuracy and efficiency, establishing it as the go-to platform for accessing information on the internet.

Under Page's leadership as CEO, Google rapidly expanded its services and became a dominant force in the tech industry. Beyond search, Google introduced a plethora of innovative products and services, including Gmail, Google Maps, Google Earth, and Google Drive, among others. Page's focus on user experience and data-driven decision-making ensured that Google's products remained at the forefront of technological innovation, delivering enhanced functionality and convenience to users worldwide.

In 2015, Page played a pivotal role in the reorganization of Google's corporate structure, establishing Alphabet Inc. as the parent company overseeing Google and its various subsidiaries. This move allowed for greater focus and autonomy in developing ambitious projects and moonshot ventures, such as Waymo (autonomous vehicles) and Verily (life sciences), while Google continued to evolve as a tech powerhouse.

Page's entrepreneurial journey has not been without challenges. Balancing innovation with the demands of a rapidly growing organization, he faced the need to streamline operations, address privacy concerns, and navigate complex global regulatory landscapes. Despite these hurdles, Page's leadership style, characterized by a long-term vision, willingness to take calculated risks, and an emphasis on technological advancements, has guided Google's continued growth and influence.

Beyond Google and Alphabet, Page's impact extends to his philanthropic endeavors. In 2010, he and his wife, Lucy Southworth, launched the Page Foundation, dedicated to supporting educational, environmental, and healthcare initiatives. Their commitment to leveraging their resources for positive change underscores Page's belief in the power of technology to improve lives and contribute to the greater good.

Larry Page's entrepreneurial journey embodies the transformative power of innovation and information. His relentless pursuit of organizing the world's knowledge and making it universally accessible has not only shaped the way we navigate the digital realm but has also ushered in a new era of connectivity, collaboration, and boundless possibilities.

As we delve into the story of Larry Page, we witness the triumphs, challenges, and the profound impact he has made on the way we access and utilize information. His visionary leadership, relentless pursuit of technological advancement, and dedication to leveraging technology for societal benefit serve as a testament to the transformative potential of entrepreneurship in the digital age.

Larry Page's legacy will forever be intertwined with the information age, as he has fundamentally reshaped the way we seek knowledge, connect with others, and navigate the vast digital landscape. His journey inspires us to embrace innovation, push boundaries, and explore the endless possibilities that lie within the realm of information and technology.

5. Sergei Brin

It is impossible to think of Sergey Brin without thinking of innovation, technological brilliance, and the unrelenting pursuit of knowledge. As the co-founder of Google alongside Larry Page, Brin has played an instrumental role in shaping the digital landscape, revolutionizing online search, and ushering in an era of boundless information accessibility. His journey as an entrepreneur and technologist exemplifies the power of curiosity, collaboration, and a steadfast commitment to pushing the boundaries of what is possible.

Born in Moscow, Russia, in 1973, Brin's passion for technology and exploration emerged at a young age. He moved to the United States with his family at the age of six, eventually enrolling at Stanford University, where he met Larry Page. The duo's shared vision for organizing the vast amount of information on the internet laid the foundation for the creation of Google.

In 1998, Brin and Page introduced the world to Google, an innovative search engine that leveraged their groundbreaking PageRank algorithm. This algorithm revolutionized the way information was retrieved on the internet by ranking web pages based on relevance and popularity. Google quickly became the go-to search engine, surpassing its competitors and providing users with an intuitive and efficient way to access information.

Under Brin's leadership, Google expanded its offerings beyond search, introducing groundbreaking products and services that have become integral to our digital lives. Brin's technical expertise and deep understanding of user needs played a crucial role in the development of products like Google Maps, Google Earth, and Google News, which further solidified Google's position as a technology leader.

Beyond Google's success, Brin's visionary thinking extended to ambitious projects that pushed the boundaries of innovation. He played a key role in the creation of Google X, a research and development division focused on moonshot projects, including the development of self-driving cars (now under Waymo) and Google Glass, a wearable augmented reality device.

Brin's entrepreneurial journey has been marked by a relentless pursuit of knowledge and a commitment to creating a culture of innovation. He understood the importance of fostering a collaborative environment that encouraged intellectual curiosity and free thinking. This philosophy was exemplified by Google's famous "20% time" policy, which allowed employees to dedicate a portion of their work hours to pursuing their own passion projects, fostering a culture of creativity and experimentation.

Throughout his career, Brin has faced challenges and navigated complex issues surrounding privacy, ethical considerations, and the responsibility of managing a vast amount of user data. However, his commitment to transparency, user trust, and constantly improving Google's products and services has been unwavering.

Brin's impact extends beyond the realm of technology and business. His philanthropic endeavors, including the establishment of the Brin Wojcicki Foundation, reflect his dedication to addressing global challenges through education, healthcare, and scientific research. He has actively supported initiatives aimed at advancing knowledge and improving lives, demonstrating his belief in the transformative power of technology for the betterment of society.

Sergey Brin's journey as an entrepreneur and innovator serves as a testament to the transformative potential of curiosity, collaboration, and a deep understanding of user needs. His technical brilliance, coupled with a visionary mindset, has reshaped the digital landscape, making information more accessible and empowering individuals worldwide.

As we explore the remarkable story of Sergey Brin, we witness the triumphs, challenges, and the profound impact he has had on the way we access, organize, and interact with information. His journey inspires us to embrace our innate curiosity, challenge the status quo, and pursue innovation that can shape the world in profound ways. Sergey Brin's relentless pursuit of knowledge and his commitment to pushing the boundaries of technology continue to inspire future generations of entrepreneurs and technologists to reimagine what is possible in the digital age.

6. Bill Gates

Bill Gates: a name that epitomizes the intersection of technological innovation, entrepreneurial genius, and philanthropic impact. From co-founding Microsoft to his remarkable journey as a business magnate and humanitarian, Gates's story is one of unparalleled vision, tenacity, and an unwavering commitment to using technology for positive change. His transformative influence has shaped the world of personal computing, redefined the concept of philanthropy, and left an indelible mark on society.

Born in Seattle, Washington, in 1955, Gates demonstrated an early affinity for programming and a keen interest in computer science. As a young teenager, he honed his skills by coding and exploring the nascent world of computing. Gates's brilliance and passion eventually led him to Harvard University, where he met Paul Allen, with whom he co-founded Microsoft in 1975.

Gates's entrepreneurial journey truly took flight with the development of the Microsoft Disk Operating System (MS-DOS), the software that laid the foundation for the personal computer revolution. Through strategic partnerships and relentless innovation, Gates propelled Microsoft to become the dominant force in the software industry, introducing iconic products such as Windows and Microsoft Office, which have become integral to millions of users around the world.

Gates's visionary leadership and business acumen were instrumental in establishing Microsoft as a global powerhouse. His foresight in recognizing the potential of the graphical user interface and the importance of user-friendly software revolutionized the way people interacted with computers. Gates's relentless pursuit of excellence, attention to detail, and ability to anticipate market trends enabled Microsoft to maintain its dominance and expand into various technological domains.

Beyond his success as a tech titan, Gates's entrepreneurial journey took a transformative turn with his transition from the corporate world to philanthropy. In 2000, Gates and his wife, Melinda Gates, established the Bill & Melinda Gates Foundation, a philanthropic organization dedicated to addressing global challenges in education, healthcare, and poverty alleviation. Through the foundation, Gates has committed substantial resources, knowledge, and influence to improve lives and drive meaningful change on a global scale.

Gates's approach to philanthropy is characterized by a data-driven mindset, a focus on innovation, and a dedication to maximizing impact. The foundation's initiatives have tackled critical issues such as global health, agricultural development, and access to education, bringing about transformative outcomes and saving countless lives around the world.

Gates's dedication to making a difference extends beyond financial contributions. He has actively used his platform and influence to raise awareness about pressing global issues, advocate for equitable access to healthcare and education, and rally leaders and governments to prioritize investments in the betterment of society.

While Gates's impact as a business magnate and philanthropist is undeniable, his journey has not been without challenges. Antitrust lawsuits, market competition, and criticism of Microsoft's business practices have tested his leadership. Nevertheless, Gates's ability to adapt, learn from setbacks, and maintain a long-term vision has allowed him to navigate the complexities of the tech industry and emerge as a revered figure.

Bill Gates's entrepreneurial journey serves as a testament to the transformative power of technology, innovation, and strategic philanthropy. His dedication to pushing the boundaries of what is possible, both in business and in addressing societal challenges, has left an indelible legacy.

As we explore the remarkable story of Bill Gates, we witness the triumphs, challenges, and the profound impact he has had on the world of technology and philanthropy. Gates's entrepreneurial spirit, visionary mindset, and commitment to using his resources and influence for the greater good continue to inspire generations of entrepreneurs, technologists, and philanthropists to harness the power of technology and drive positive change in the world.

7. Steve Jobs

Steve Jobs: a name that evokes images of revolutionary products, cutting-edge design, and unwavering commitment to excellence. As the co-founder of Apple Inc., Jobs left an indelible mark on the world of technology and consumer electronics. His entrepreneurial journey was defined by his relentless pursuit of perfection, visionary thinking, and the ability to transform industries through innovation.

Born in San Francisco, California, in 1955, Jobs was exposed to the world of electronics and technology from a young age. His passion for computer science and design led him to co-found Apple Inc. in 1976, along with Steve Wozniak. Together, they ignited a revolution that would redefine personal computing and shape the digital landscape.

Under Jobs's leadership, Apple introduced groundbreaking products that became cultural icons and pushed the boundaries of innovation. The release of the Apple II in 1977 and the Macintosh in 1984 showcased Jobs's vision for intuitive user interfaces and elegant design. These products transformed the way people interacted with computers, making them more accessible and user-friendly.

Despite his initial departure from Apple in 1985, Jobs's entrepreneurial spirit and unwavering commitment to innovation led him to establish NeXT Inc., a computer hardware and software company. NeXT's focus on cutting-edge technology and design laid the groundwork for Jobs's eventual return to Apple in 1997 when Apple acquired NeXT. This marked the beginning of Jobs's triumphant second act at Apple.

With his return, Jobs embarked on a transformative journey that would redefine Apple's trajectory and propel it to unprecedented heights. Under his leadership as CEO, Apple introduced a string of game-changing products, starting with the iMac in 1998, followed by the iPod, iPhone, and iPad. Jobs's insistence on seamless integration of hardware and software, minimalist design, and unparalleled user experience made these products not just devices but coveted lifestyle accessories.

Jobs's ability to anticipate and shape consumer desires was exemplified by his ability to create entirely new product categories. The iPhone, released in 2007, revolutionized the mobile industry by combining a touch screen interface, multimedia capabilities, and internet connectivity into a single device. This visionary approach transformed the way we communicate, consume media, and access information.

Beyond his impact on technology, Jobs's keen eye for design and branding extended to the retail space. The Apple Stores, with their minimalist aesthetics and immersive customer experiences, revolutionized the concept of retail, showcasing Jobs's ability to seamlessly integrate hardware, software, and physical spaces.

Jobs's entrepreneurial journey was not without challenges. His pursuit of perfection and his demanding leadership style earned him a reputation for being difficult to work with. However, his relentless pursuit of excellence and his unwavering belief in his vision allowed him to overcome setbacks and inspire those around him to achieve greatness.

Steve Jobs's impact extended beyond Apple. His influence reached the realms of animation, music, and publishing through his acquisition of Pixar Animation Studios, his involvement with the creation of iTunes and the App Store, and his leadership in transforming the music and publishing industries.

Jobs's entrepreneurial journey serves as a testament to the power of innovation, design, and the relentless pursuit of excellence. His ability to envision products that transcended mere functionality and became extensions of our lives set him apart as a visionary. His passion for pushing the boundaries of what is possible and his commitment to creating products that enrich and enhance the lives of users continue to inspire generations of entrepreneurs and designers.

As we delve into the remarkable story of Steve Jobs, we witness the triumphs, challenges, and the profound impact he had on the world of technology and consumer electronics. Jobs's unwavering belief in the power of design, his ability to anticipate consumer needs, and his uncompromising pursuit of perfection continue to shape the way we interact with technology and define what is possible in the digital age.

8. Jack Dorsey

Jack Dorsey: a name synonymous with social networking, real-time communication, and the power of concise expression. As the co-founder of Twitter, Dorsey has left an indelible mark on the way we connect, share information, and engage with the world. His entrepreneurial journey has been defined by his vision for open communication, innovation in technology, and a commitment to fostering global conversations.

Born in St. Louis, Missouri, in 1976, Dorsey displayed a keen interest in programming and technology from an early age. His fascination with communication systems and his vision for a platform that would enable people to share thoughts and ideas in real-time laid the foundation for the creation of Twitter.

In 2006, Dorsey, along with his co-founders, introduced Twitter, a microblogging platform that revolutionized social media and transformed the way we communicate. With its iconic 280-character limit, Twitter provided a platform for users to express themselves concisely and engage in conversations that transcended geographic boundaries. The simplicity and immediacy of Twitter's format fueled its rapid growth and established it as a powerful tool for news, information dissemination, and social interaction.

Under Dorsey's leadership, Twitter continued to evolve and

introduce new features, such as hashtags, retweets, and verified accounts, that shaped the way users engage with content and connect with others. Dorsey's emphasis on real-time information and the democratization of communication empowered individuals to have a voice on a global scale, facilitating conversations that spanned industries, cultures, and communities.

Dorsey's entrepreneurial journey extended beyond Twitter. In 2009, he founded Square, a mobile payment company that revolutionized small business transactions. Square's innovative card reader and accompanying software made it possible for small merchants to accept credit card payments easily, disrupting traditional payment systems and empowering entrepreneurs worldwide.

Despite his notable achievements, Dorsey's journey has been marked by challenges and controversies. As CEO of Twitter, he faced the daunting task of managing the platform's growth, addressing issues such as online harassment and misinformation, and navigating complex debates surrounding free speech and censorship. Through it all, Dorsey's commitment to open dialogue and continuous improvement has driven Twitter's evolution as a platform that facilitates meaningful conversations while tackling the challenges associated with its scale and influence.

Beyond his contributions to technology and social media, Dorsey has also been involved in various philanthropic endeavors. He has pledged a significant portion of his wealth to causes such as education, healthcare, and universal basic income. Dorsey's commitment to using his resources for societal good reflects his belief in the power of technology to create positive change and address pressing global challenges.

Jack Dorsey's entrepreneurial journey embodies the transformative power of social connection and the democratization of communication. His vision for Twitter and Square, coupled with his commitment to innovation and meaningful dialogue, has reshaped the way we engage with information, express ourselves, and conduct business.

As we delve into the remarkable story of Jack Dorsey, we witness the triumphs, challenges, and the profound impact he has had on the way we connect and communicate in the digital age. Dorsey's commitment to fostering global conversations, enabling concise expression, and leveraging technology for positive change continues to inspire individuals, entrepreneurs, and social activists around the world to embrace the power of open communication and harness the potential of technology to shape a more connected and inclusive world.

9. Reid Hoffman

As the co-founder of LinkedIn, Reid Hoffman has played a pivotal role in revolutionizing the way professionals connect, build relationships, and advance their careers. His entrepreneurial journey has been marked by a deep understanding of social dynamics, a commitment to fostering innovation, and a passion for empowering individuals in the professional realm.

Born in Stanford, California, in 1967, Hoffman's fascination with technology and human interaction emerged at an early age. He pursued his passion by studying Symbolic Systems at Stanford University, exploring the intersections of computer science, cognitive psychology, and philosophy. This multidisciplinary background laid the foundation for his future endeavors in the tech industry.

In 2002, Hoffman co-founded LinkedIn, a professional networking platform that transformed the way professionals connect, share expertise, and seek opportunities. LinkedIn provided a digital space for individuals to showcase their professional accomplishments, expand their networks, and access career resources. With its emphasis on authenticity, credibility, and meaningful connections, LinkedIn quickly gained traction and became an indispensable tool for professionals worldwide.

Under Hoffman's leadership, LinkedIn evolved into a thriving ecosystem that goes beyond traditional networking. The platform introduced features such as job listings, professional groups, and content publishing, empowering individuals to not only connect but also learn, collaborate, and showcase their expertise. This holistic approach to professional networking transformed LinkedIn into a dynamic hub for career development and industry insights.

Hoffman's entrepreneurial journey extends beyond LinkedIn. As a venture capitalist, he has been instrumental in shaping the trajectory of numerous successful companies. His involvement in ventures such as PayPal, Airbnb, and Facebook has not only solidified his reputation as a savvy investor but has also allowed him to mentor and support the next generation of entrepreneurs. Hoffman's insights, strategic guidance, and belief in the power of networks have helped emerging startups navigate the complexities of the business world and achieve success.

In addition to his contributions in the business realm, Hoffman is a strong advocate for social impact and the democratization of opportunities. He has co-authored books on entrepreneurship and career strategies, sharing valuable insights and practical advice with aspiring professionals. Hoffman's commitment to empowering individuals to reach their full potential transcends the professional realm, as he actively engages in initiatives that address social challenges and promote equitable access to education and economic opportunities.

Hoffman's impact extends to the realm of thought leadership and public discourse. He is known for his insightful commentary on the future of work, the role of technology in society, and the importance of fostering resilient networks. His ability to anticipate trends, envision new possibilities, and articulate them to a wider audience has earned him respect as a visionary thought leader.

Reid Hoffman's entrepreneurial journey serves as a testament to the transformative power of professional networking, mentorship, and the pursuit of social impact. His vision for LinkedIn, combined with his deep understanding of human connections, has reshaped the way professionals navigate their careers and build meaningful relationships in the digital age.

As we explore the remarkable story of Reid Hoffman, we witness the triumphs, challenges, and the profound impact he has had on the world of professional networking and entrepreneurship. Hoffman's commitment to fostering innovation, empowering individuals, and leveraging technology to create positive change continues to inspire professionals, entrepreneurs, and aspiring changemakers around the world to embrace the power of connections and seize opportunities in an interconnected global landscape.

10. Travis Kalanick

As the co-founder of Uber, Travis Kalanick has forever changed the landscape of transportation and redefined the way we think about mobility. His entrepreneurial journey has been characterized by audacious disruption, relentless ambition, and a determination to revolutionize an industry ripe for change.

Born in Los Angeles, California, in 1976, Kalanick displayed an entrepreneurial spirit from a young age. He ventured into the tech world early on, co-founding several startups before embarking on his most notable endeavor - Uber. In 2009, Kalanick, along with Garrett Camp, introduced a game-changing concept: a ride-hailing service that leveraged technology to connect drivers and passengers seamlessly.

Under Kalanick's leadership, Uber quickly gained traction and disrupted the traditional taxi industry. The convenience, affordability, and reliability offered by the Uber platform made it an attractive alternative to traditional transportation options. Kalanick's relentless focus on innovation, coupled with his ability to mobilize resources and navigate regulatory challenges, propelled Uber to become a global phenomenon, transforming the way people commute in cities around the world.

Kalanick's vision for Uber extended beyond ride-hailing. He

recognized the potential of leveraging technology to unlock new possibilities in other industries, leading to the introduction of services such as UberEATS and Uber Freight. These expansions showcased Kalanick's ambition to create a comprehensive platform that catered to various aspects of transportation and logistics.

However, Kalanick's journey as the CEO of Uber was not without controversy. The company faced numerous allegations, including issues related to workplace culture, regulatory compliance, and competitive practices. Kalanick's leadership style, characterized by an aggressive and relentless pursuit of growth, drew criticism and scrutiny. These challenges ultimately led to his departure from Uber in 2017.

Despite the controversies, Kalanick's impact on the transportation industry and the concept of the sharing economy remains undeniable. Uber's disruptive influence inspired the emergence of numerous ride-hailing and mobility startups, transforming the way we think about transportation and challenging traditional business models.

Following his departure from Uber, Kalanick continued his entrepreneurial pursuits and venture capital investments. He launched CloudKitchens, a company focused on providing shared kitchen spaces to food delivery businesses, embracing the evolving demands of the restaurant industry. Kalanick's ability to identify emerging market trends and capitalize on opportunities demonstrates his entrepreneurial acumen and adaptability.

Travis Kalanick's entrepreneurial journey embodies the spirit of disruptive innovation and the pursuit of transformation. His vision for Uber and his unwavering determination to challenge the status quo have reshaped the transportation industry and inspired a new wave of entrepreneurial ventures. Kalanick's ability to leverage technology to solve complex problems and create new business models exemplifies the power of entrepreneurship to drive societal change.

As we delve into the remarkable story of Travis Kalanick, we witness the triumphs, challenges, and the profound impact he has had on the world of transportation and entrepreneurship. Kalanick's disruptive mindset, audacious ambition, and relentless pursuit of innovation continue to inspire entrepreneurs, industry leaders, and changemakers to challenge norms, embrace change, and transform industries through the power of technology and entrepreneurial vision.

11. Evan Spiegel

As the co-founder and CEO of Snapchat, Evan Spiegel has left an indelible mark on the world of social media, capturing the attention of millions with his unique vision and commitment to user-centric experiences. His entrepreneurial journey has been characterized by a relentless pursuit of reinvention, an unwavering belief in the power of storytelling, and a dedication to creating platforms that celebrate authenticity and self-expression.

Born in Los Angeles, California, in 1990, Spiegel's passion for technology and design was evident from an early age. He pursued his studies at Stanford University, where he crossed paths with his future co-founders and embarked on the journey of creating what would become one of the most influential social media platforms of our time - Snapchat.

In 2011, Spiegel and his team introduced Snapchat, a mobile application that revolutionized the way we communicate and share moments. At its core, Snapchat disrupted the traditional model of social media by introducing the concept of ephemeral messaging, where photos and videos would disappear after being viewed. This unique approach resonated with users, particularly younger generations, who sought more private, authentic, and in-the-moment connections.

Under Spiegel's leadership, Snapchat continued to innovate and introduce new features that differentiated it from other social media platforms. The introduction of Stories, which allowed users to share a collection of photos and videos that would disappear after 24 hours, further propelled Snapchat's growth and engagement. This format not only captured the essence of storytelling but also provided a platform for users to express themselves in a more candid and unfiltered manner.

Spiegel's commitment to innovation and user experience extended beyond Snapchat. The introduction of augmented reality (AR) features, such as Lenses and Filters, added a playful and interactive element to the platform, transforming the way users engage with content and express their creativity. These AR experiences not only entertained but also opened doors for brands, advertisers, and content creators to engage with audiences in new and immersive ways.

Despite facing fierce competition from other social media giants, Spiegel's ability to stay true to Snapchat's unique identity and continually evolve its offerings has helped the platform maintain its relevance and attract a loyal user base. Spiegel's forward-thinking approach and willingness to take risks have allowed Snapchat to redefine the social media landscape and inspire new avenues of creative expression.

Outside of his work at Snapchat, Spiegel is known for his philanthropic efforts and commitment to social impact. He has focused on initiatives related to education, youth empowerment, and community development, aiming to make a positive difference in the lives of young people around the world.

Evan Spiegel's entrepreneurial journey exemplifies the power of innovation, authenticity, and self-expression in shaping the world of social media. His vision for Snapchat, coupled with his unwavering commitment to user-centric experiences and storytelling, has transformed the way we connect, communicate, and share our lives with others.

As we explore the remarkable story of Evan Spiegel, we witness the triumphs, challenges, and the profound impact he has had on the world of social media and digital communication. Spiegel's relentless pursuit of reinvention, his dedication to celebrating authenticity, and his commitment to empowering users to express themselves continue to inspire individuals, content creators, and entrepreneurs to embrace their unique stories, push boundaries, and redefine the future of social media.

12. Brian Chesky

As the co-founder and CEO of Airbnb, Brian Chesky has transformed the hospitality industry, empowering individuals to become hosts and travelers to immerse themselves in unique and authentic experiences. His entrepreneurial journey has been defined by a passion for design, a commitment to creating a sense of belonging, and a dedication to fostering human connections.

Born in Niskayuna, New York, in 1981, Chesky's early interests in art and design laid the groundwork for his future endeavors. He pursued his studies at the Rhode Island School of Design, where he developed a deep appreciation for the intersection of creativity and functionality. This foundation would prove instrumental in shaping his approach to entrepreneurship and product development.

In 2008, Chesky, along with his co-founders, introduced Airbnb, a platform that revolutionized the way people travel and experience destinations. Airbnb allowed individuals to rent out their homes or spare rooms, providing travelers with unique accommodations and the opportunity to connect with local hosts. This novel approach disrupted the traditional hotel industry and tapped into the growing desire for more personalized, authentic travel experiences.

Under Chesky's leadership, Airbnb expanded its offerings beyond just accommodation. The introduction of Experiences allowed hosts to share their passions and expertise with travelers, curating one-of-a-kind activities and immersions in local culture. This emphasis on experiential travel provided a platform for individuals to connect, learn from one another, and foster a sense of community across borders.

Chesky's commitment to design and user experience elevated Airbnb to new heights. The platform's intuitive interface, coupled with its emphasis on trust, safety, and community, established it as a trusted marketplace for both hosts and guests. Chesky's attention to detail, from the quality of listings to the overall aesthetic of the brand, contributed to the creation of a seamless and memorable user experience.

Throughout his journey, Chesky has faced challenges and navigated complex issues. Airbnb has encountered regulatory hurdles, concerns around safety and security, and the impact of the COVID-19 pandemic on the travel industry. However, Chesky's ability to adapt, listen to feedback, and innovate has allowed Airbnb to overcome obstacles and emerge as a resilient global brand.

Chesky's impact extends beyond the realm of travel. He has championed the idea of belonging and community, emphasizing the role of Airbnb in fostering connections and understanding among people from diverse backgrounds. His commitment to corporate social responsibility has seen Airbnb engage in initiatives related to affordable housing, disaster response, and environmental sustainability.

Brian Chesky's entrepreneurial journey showcases the transformative power of experiential travel and the importance of human connections in the digital age. His vision for Airbnb, combined with his passion for design and commitment to fostering a sense of belonging, has redefined the way we travel and experience the world.

As we delve into the remarkable story of Brian Chesky, we witness the triumphs, challenges, and the profound impact he has had on the travel industry and the way we connect with others. Chesky's

45

dedication to creating meaningful experiences, his focus on community building, and his belief in the power of travel to bridge divides continue to inspire travelers, hosts, and entrepreneurs to embrace new possibilities, celebrate cultural diversity, and forge lasting connections through the transformative power of experiential travel.

13. Kevin Systrom

As the co-founder of Instagram, Kevin Systrom has reshaped the way we capture, share, and experience moments through the lens of a camera. His entrepreneurial journey is marked by a keen eye for design, a passion for photography, and a commitment to building a platform that celebrates visual expression.

Born in Holliston, Massachusetts, in 1983, Systrom's fascination with technology and art began at an early age. He pursued his studies at Stanford University, where he honed his technical skills while nurturing his passion for photography. This unique combination of interests laid the foundation for the creation of a platform that would redefine the way we engage with images.

In 2010, Systrom and his co-founder, Mike Krieger, introduced Instagram, a mobile application that allowed users to capture and share photos instantly. Instagram's intuitive interface and powerful editing tools democratized the world of photography, enabling users to capture and enhance their moments with ease. The platform's emphasis on simplicity, visual aesthetics, and social interaction resonated with users and propelled its rapid growth.

Under Systrom's leadership, Instagram evolved beyond a mere photo-sharing app. The introduction of filters and editing features gave users the ability to transform ordinary photos into visually captivating works of art. This approach democratized creativity and empowered individuals to express themselves through imagery, regardless of their level of expertise.

As Instagram gained popularity, Systrom recognized the power of community and engagement. The introduction of features like hashtags, comments, and likes facilitated meaningful interactions between users, sparking conversations and forging connections around shared interests. Instagram became more than just a platform for photo sharing; it became a global community of visual storytellers.

In 2012, Instagram caught the attention of Facebook, and Systrom made the decision to sell the platform to the social media giant. This acquisition allowed Instagram to tap into Facebook's vast user base and resources while maintaining its distinct identity and creative culture.

Under Systrom's continued leadership within Instagram, the platform continued to innovate and expand its offerings. The introduction of Instagram Stories, a feature inspired by Snapchat's ephemeral content, provided users with a new way to share moments in a more spontaneous and authentic manner. This feature quickly gained traction, further solidifying Instagram's position as a leading social media platform.

Throughout his journey, Systrom has emphasized the importance of authenticity and user experience. He has actively engaged with the Instagram community, listening to feedback and implementing changes to improve the platform. His commitment to user privacy and safety has driven the implementation of features to combat online harassment and ensure a positive user experience.

Kevin Systrom's entrepreneurial journey exemplifies the power of visual storytelling and the democratization of creativity. His vision for Instagram, coupled with his appreciation for design and photography, has transformed the way we engage with images and share our stories.

As we explore the remarkable story of Kevin Systrom, we witness the triumphs, challenges, and the profound impact he has had on the world of social media and visual expression. Systrom's dedication to simplicity, his commitment to community building, and his belief in the power of visual communication continue to inspire photographers, content creators, and individuals around the world to embrace their creativity, capture meaningful moments, and share their unique perspectives through the captivating lens of Instagram.

14. Jan Koum

As the co-founder of WhatsApp, Jan Koum has played a pivotal role in revolutionizing the way we communicate and connect with others across borders. His entrepreneurial journey is marked by perseverance, a commitment to privacy, and a passion for providing a simple, reliable, and secure messaging platform.

Born in Ukraine in 1976, Koum's childhood was marked by adversity and economic challenges. In 1992, he immigrated to the United States with his mother, seeking better opportunities. This experience shaped Koum's outlook on life and instilled in him a strong work ethic and determination to succeed.

Koum's passion for technology became evident at a young age. While working at Yahoo as an infrastructure engineer, he identified a gap in the communication landscape: the need for a secure and reliable messaging platform that transcended traditional SMS limitations. In 2009, Koum, along with his co-founder Brian Acton, introduced WhatsApp, a cross-platform messaging application that offered an alternative to costly SMS services.

At the heart of WhatsApp's success lies Koum's commitment to simplicity and user experience. The app's clean interface, efficient messaging capabilities, and focus on end-to-end encryption quickly attracted millions of users worldwide. WhatsApp's low-cost, real-time communication capabilities made it particularly appealing in emerging markets, where traditional SMS services were often prohibitively expensive.

Koum's dedication to privacy and security has been a driving force behind WhatsApp's development. By implementing end-to-end encryption, WhatsApp ensures that messages remain private and secure, giving users peace of mind in their digital interactions. This commitment to protecting user data has been integral to WhatsApp's popularity and continued growth.

In 2014, Facebook acquired WhatsApp, recognizing its immense value as a global communication platform. Koum continued to lead WhatsApp within the Facebook ecosystem, ensuring its autonomy and commitment to user privacy. Under his guidance, WhatsApp expanded its offerings, introducing voice and video calling features, group chats, and business messaging solutions.

Beyond his role at WhatsApp, Koum is known for his philanthropic efforts. He has dedicated resources to support causes close to his heart, including education and community development. His personal journey as an immigrant has influenced his desire to make a positive impact and empower individuals around the world.

Jan Koum's entrepreneurial journey exemplifies the transformative power of messaging and the importance of privacy in our interconnected world. His vision for WhatsApp, coupled with his unwavering commitment to simplicity and security, has revolutionized the way we communicate, breaking down barriers and bringing people closer together.

As we delve into the remarkable story of Jan Koum, we witness the triumphs, challenges, and the profound impact he has had on the world of messaging and global connectivity. Koum's dedication to user privacy, his relentless pursuit of simplicity, and his belief in the power of technology to bridge gaps continue to inspire individuals, businesses, and communities to embrace the possibilities of communication and forge meaningful connections through the innovative platform of WhatsApp.

15. Drew Houston

As the co-founder and CEO of Dropbox, Drew Houston has revolutionized the way we store, access, and collaborate on files in the digital age. His entrepreneurial journey is marked by a relentless pursuit of simplicity, a passion for user-centric design, and a commitment to empowering individuals and businesses to work more efficiently.

Born in Acton, Massachusetts, in 1983, Houston showed an early aptitude for technology and programming. He pursued his studies at the Massachusetts Institute of Technology (MIT), where he further honed his technical skills and developed a deep understanding of the challenges individuals faced in managing their digital files.

Inspired by the frustration of constantly forgetting his USB drive, Houston set out to create a solution that would make file storage and sharing effortless. In 2007, he co-founded Dropbox, a cloud storage platform that allows users to store, synchronize, and share files across multiple devices seamlessly.

At the core of Dropbox's success lies Houston's commitment to simplicity and user experience. The platform's intuitive interface, coupled with its powerful syncing capabilities, transformed the way individuals and teams collaborate on projects. Dropbox's seamless integration into existing workflows made it a go-to solution for professionals, creatives, and businesses of all sizes.

Houston's relentless pursuit of innovation led to the introduction of new features and functionalities that enhanced the productivity of Dropbox users. The integration of collaborative tools, such as shared folders and file commenting, allowed for real-time collaboration, enabling teams to work together efficiently regardless of their physical location.

Under Houston's leadership, Dropbox expanded its offerings beyond file storage. The introduction of Dropbox Paper, a collaborative workspace for teams, provided a platform for creating and sharing documents, notes, and project plans in a seamless and collaborative manner. This expansion showcased Houston's commitment to empowering individuals and teams with the tools they need to unleash their creative potential.

Houston's emphasis on user privacy and security has been a driving force behind Dropbox's development. He has prioritized the protection of user data, implementing robust encryption and security measures to ensure the privacy and integrity of files stored on the platform. This dedication to user trust has played a crucial role in establishing Dropbox as a trusted name in cloud storage.

Beyond his role at Dropbox, Houston has been an advocate for entrepreneurship and the power of technology to drive positive change. He has mentored aspiring entrepreneurs and actively supports initiatives that promote diversity and inclusion in the tech industry.

Drew Houston's entrepreneurial journey exemplifies the transformative power of cloud storage and collaboration. His vision for Dropbox, coupled with his commitment to simplicity and user-centric design, has redefined the way individuals and teams work, collaborate, and share digital content.

As we explore the remarkable story of Drew Houston, we witness the triumphs, challenges, and the profound impact he has had on the world of productivity and file management. Houston's dedication to simplicity, his relentless pursuit of innovation, and his belief in the power of technology to empower individuals continue to inspire professionals, businesses, and creative minds to embrace the possibilities of digital collaboration and productivity through the innovative platform of Dropbox.

16. Peter Thiel

Peter Thiel: a name synonymous with innovation, contrarian thinking, and groundbreaking investments. As a venture capitalist, entrepreneur, and author, Thiel has left an indelible mark on the technology industry and the startup ecosystem. His entrepreneurial journey is defined by a bold vision, a relentless pursuit of disruption, and a commitment to transforming industries through technological advancements.

Born in Frankfurt, Germany, in 1967, Thiel moved to the United States at an early age. He studied philosophy at Stanford University and later pursued a law degree at Stanford Law School. Thiel's multidisciplinary background, coupled with his deep interest in technology and finance, set the stage for his future endeavors.

In 1998, Thiel co-founded PayPal, an online payment platform that revolutionized the way individuals and businesses transact online. PayPal's success and subsequent acquisition by eBay established Thiel as a prominent figure in the technology industry. This early triumph showcased Thiel's ability to identify disruptive opportunities and leverage technology to transform traditional industries.

As a venture capitalist, Thiel co-founded Founders Fund, a venture capital firm known for its contrarian investment strategies. Thiel's investment philosophy is characterized by a focus on bold ideas and transformative technologies. He has been an early investor in companies such as Facebook, SpaceX, Airbnb, and Palantir Technologies, among others, cementing his reputation as a visionary investor.

Thiel's contrarian thinking extends beyond investments. In 2012, he published the book "Zero to One," where he shares his insights on startups and innovation. Thiel challenges conventional wisdom, advocating for the pursuit of unique, game-changing ideas that have the potential to create new markets or dominate existing ones. This contrarian mindset has inspired entrepreneurs and innovators to think differently and embrace the risks and rewards of groundbreaking innovation.

Thiel's influence and impact extend beyond his investments and writings. He is known for his outspoken views on various topics, including the role of technology in society and the importance of individual liberty. Thiel's contrarian perspectives have sparked debates and discussions, pushing the boundaries of conventional thinking and challenging the status quo.

Thiel's commitment to technological advancement is exemplified by his involvement with the Thiel Fellowship, a program that supports young entrepreneurs by offering financial support and mentorship to pursue their ambitious projects. This initiative reflects Thiel's belief in the power of youth and the potential for disruptive innovation to reshape industries and drive societal progress.

Peter Thiel's entrepreneurial journey exemplifies the transformative power of disruptive thinking and the importance of embracing contrarian perspectives. His vision for groundbreaking technologies, coupled with his bold investments and contrarian views, has reshaped industries, inspired entrepreneurs, and challenged the way we think about innovation.

As we delve into the remarkable story of Peter Thiel, we witness the triumphs, challenges, and the profound impact he has had on the technology industry and the startup ecosystem. Thiel's dedication to bold ideas, his relentless pursuit of disruption, and his belief in the power of technology to shape the future continue to inspire entrepreneurs, investors, and innovators to think beyond the boundaries of what is possible and strive for transformative change in the world.

17. Tim Cook

Tim Cook, born on November 1, 1960, in Mobile, Alabama, is an American business executive who rose to prominence as the CEO of Apple Inc., succeeding the legendary Steve Jobs. Cook's story is a testament to his exceptional leadership, strategic vision, and unwavering commitment to innovation.

Before joining Apple, Cook built an impressive career in the technology industry. After earning his bachelor's degree in Industrial Engineering from Auburn University in 1982, he joined the computer technology company IBM. Cook quickly established himself as a skilled operations executive, demonstrating a keen understanding of supply chain management and logistics.

In 1998, Cook left IBM to join Apple at a crucial juncture in the company's history. At the time, Apple was facing significant challenges and struggling to regain its market position. Cook's expertise in streamlining operations and optimizing supply chains proved instrumental in transforming Apple's manufacturing and distribution processes.

Cook's contributions did not go unnoticed, and he quickly ascended the ranks at Apple. In 2004, he was appointed as the Executive Vice President of Worldwide Sales and Operations, assuming greater responsibility for Apple's global operations and supply chain management.

When Steve Jobs took a medical leave of absence in 2009, Cook was named the interim CEO. During this period, Cook skillfully led Apple and kept the company on track, earning the admiration and trust of both employees and stakeholders. His ability to steer Apple successfully through a challenging phase cemented his reputation as a capable leader.

In 2011, following Steve Jobs' resignation as CEO, Tim Cook was officially named Apple's CEO. Under Cook's leadership, Apple experienced unprecedented growth and continued to push the boundaries of technology and design. Cook's strategic decisions and customer-centric approach guided Apple's product development, expanding its range to include iconic devices like the iPhone, iPad, and Apple Watch.

Beyond product innovation, Cook has championed important initiatives at Apple, focusing on environmental sustainability, social responsibility, and privacy. Under his guidance, Apple has made significant strides in reducing its carbon footprint, transitioning to renewable energy, and promoting diversity and inclusion within the company.

Cook's leadership style is marked by his commitment to ethical business practices, respect for privacy, and unwavering dedication to user experience. He has emphasized the importance of prioritizing customer needs, ensuring that Apple's products and services enhance people's lives and make a positive impact on society.

Throughout his tenure, Cook has faced numerous challenges, from intense competition to global economic fluctuations. However, his ability to navigate these complexities while maintaining Apple's commitment to innovation and quality has solidified his reputation as one of the most influential and successful business leaders of his time.

Beyond Apple, Cook is also known for his philanthropy and advocacy for social causes. He has been vocal on issues such as equality, privacy rights, and immigration reform, using his platform to make a positive impact on society.

Tim Cook's story is an embodiment of perseverance, strategic acumen, and an unwavering commitment to excellence. As he continues to lead Apple into the future, his legacy will be remembered as that of a visionary leader who not only transformed a company but also shaped the way we interact with technology, inspiring generations to come.

18. Larry Ellison

A name that has become firmly linked to technological mastery, inventiveness, and the dogged pursuit of one's goals is that of Larry Ellison. Ellison has left an indelible effect on the technology sector and transformed the landscape of corporate software as the co-founder and former CEO of Oracle Corporation. His contributions to these fields are indisputable. His entrepreneurial journey is characterized by a fierce competitive spirit, a penchant for disruptive innovation, and a commitment to pushing the boundaries of what's possible.

Born in New York City in 1944, Ellison's early life was marked by challenges and a strong desire to succeed. He dropped out of college twice, but his thirst for knowledge and passion for technology led him to the world of computer programming. Ellison's early career involved working on various projects, including database development, which would later become the foundation of his groundbreaking company, Oracle.

In 1977, Ellison, along with two partners, founded Software Development Laboratories, which eventually became Oracle Corporation. Ellison's vision was to develop a relational database management system that could handle vast amounts of data efficiently. This vision laid the groundwork for Oracle's rise to prominence as a leading provider of enterprise software and a key player in the technology industry.

Under Ellison's leadership, Oracle became known for its innovative products and acquisitions that expanded its portfolio and market presence. Ellison's competitive spirit and drive for success propelled Oracle to challenge and disrupt established players in the industry. His strategic acquisitions, including PeopleSoft and Sun Microsystems, strengthened Oracle's position as a comprehensive provider of enterprise solutions.

Ellison's bold approach to innovation and willingness to take risks has been a defining aspect of his entrepreneurial journey. He has championed groundbreaking technologies such as cloud computing and artificial intelligence, recognizing their potential to transform industries and drive efficiency. Ellison's unwavering belief in the power of technology to revolutionize business processes has guided Oracle's trajectory and cemented its status as an industry leader.

Beyond his role at Oracle, Ellison is known for his passion for competitive sailing. His involvement in the America's Cup, a prestigious sailing event, reflects his competitive nature and his pursuit of excellence both in business and personal endeavors. Ellison's love for sailing has also led to advancements in yacht design and technology, further demonstrating his commitment to pushing boundaries and seeking innovation in all aspects of life.

Larry Ellison's entrepreneurial journey exemplifies the transformative power of technological innovation and the drive to disrupt established norms. His vision for Oracle, coupled with his relentless pursuit of success and competitive spirit, has reshaped the enterprise software industry and set new standards for technological excellence.

As we explore the remarkable story of Larry Ellison, we witness the triumphs, challenges, and the profound impact he has had on the technology landscape. Ellison's dedication to innovation, his unwavering pursuit of success, and his belief in the transformative power of technology continue to inspire entrepreneurs, business leaders, and technologists to push the boundaries of what's possible and redefine the future of industries around the world.

19. Ben Silberman

As the co-founder and CEO of Pinterest, Ben Silberman has transformed the way millions of people discover and curate ideas online. His entrepreneurial journey is marked by a passion for design, a commitment to user experience, and a vision to create a platform that inspires and empowers individuals around the world.

Born in Des Moines, Iowa, Silberman showed an early interest in design and aesthetics. He pursued his studies at Yale University, where he studied political science but remained fascinated by the world of design and visual communication. Silberman's diverse interests and desire to create something meaningful laid the foundation for his future endeavors.

The idea for Pinterest began to take shape when Silberman and his co-founder, Evan Sharp, recognized the challenge of organizing and discovering inspiration online. They envisioned a platform where users could collect and share ideas through visual bookmarks known as "pins." In 2010, Pinterest was born, offering a new way for individuals to discover, organize, and curate content across a wide range of interests.

At the core of Pinterest's success lies Silberman's commitment to design and user experience. The platform's clean and intuitive interface, coupled with its visual-centric approach, created a unique and immersive experience for users. Silberman's belief in the power of aesthetics and the ability of visuals to inspire and connect people resonated with millions of users worldwide.

Silberman's dedication to fostering a positive and inclusive community has been instrumental in Pinterest's growth. He has placed great importance on combating misinformation, promoting mental health and well-being, and ensuring a safe and supportive environment for users. Silberman's commitment to user trust and well-being has guided Pinterest's development and solidified its reputation as a platform that values the interests and needs of its users.

Under Silberman's leadership, Pinterest has expanded its offerings and introduced innovative features. The introduction of curated recommendations, personalized feeds, and shopping capabilities have enhanced the discovery and shopping experience for users. Silberman's commitment to continuous improvement and innovation has allowed Pinterest to evolve into a versatile platform that caters to a diverse range of interests and aspirations.

Beyond his role at Pinterest, Silberman is known for his humility and his passion for helping others. He has shared his experiences and insights with aspiring entrepreneurs and has been an advocate for diversity and inclusion in the tech industry. Silberman's personal journey, combined with his belief in the power of creativity and inspiration, has inspired individuals to embrace their unique passions and pursue their dreams.

Ben Silberman's entrepreneurial journey exemplifies the transformative power of visual discovery and the importance of design in creating meaningful connections. His vision for Pinterest, coupled with his commitment to user experience and community well-being, has redefined how people discover, organize, and share inspiration online.

As we delve into the remarkable story of Ben Silberman, we witness the triumphs, challenges, and the profound impact he has had on the world of visual discovery. Silberman's dedication to design, his unwavering pursuit of user-centric experiences, and his belief in the power of inspiration continue to inspire individuals, creators, and dreamers to explore their passions, connect with others, and find endless possibilities through the innovative platform of Pinterest.

20. Reed Hastings

As the co-founder and CEO of Netflix, Reed Hastings has revolutionized the way millions of people consume and enjoy movies and television shows. His entrepreneurial journey is characterized by a forward-thinking mindset, a commitment to technological advancements, and a vision to create a global streaming platform that offers personalized, on-demand entertainment.

Born in Boston, Massachusetts, in 1960, Hastings developed an early passion for technology and entrepreneurship. He pursued his studies at Bowdoin College and later earned a master's degree in computer science from Stanford University. Hastings' deep understanding of technology and his entrepreneurial spirit set the stage for his future endeavors.

In 1997, Hastings co-founded Netflix, initially as a DVD rental-by-mail service. The idea stemmed from a personal frustration Hastings experienced when he had to pay hefty late fees for rented movies. He envisioned a platform that would eliminate late fees and provide users with a more convenient way to rent and enjoy movies at home.

Hastings' vision expanded beyond physical media as he recognized the potential of streaming technology. Under his leadership, Netflix transformed from a DVD rental service to a streaming giant, offering a vast library of movies, TV shows, and original content to subscribers worldwide. This shift disrupted the traditional video rental and broadcast industries, forever changing the way people consume entertainment.

Central to Netflix's success is Hastings' emphasis on data-driven decision-making and personalization. Netflix's recommendation algorithm, powered by machine learning and user behavior analysis, delivers tailored content suggestions to each subscriber, enhancing the viewing experience and keeping users engaged. Hastings' commitment to leveraging technology and data has positioned Netflix as a leader in the era of personalized entertainment.

Hastings' relentless pursuit of original content has been a key factor in Netflix's rise to prominence. Under his guidance, Netflix has produced critically acclaimed and award-winning original series, documentaries, and films. By investing in diverse storytelling and empowering talented creators, Hastings has built a platform that appeals to a wide range of audiences and continues to push the boundaries of what's possible in content creation.

Beyond his role at Netflix, Hastings has been an advocate for education and philanthropy. He has championed initiatives to improve educational systems and expand access to quality education. Hastings' dedication to social impact and his belief in the power of education to transform lives reflect his commitment to making a positive difference in the world beyond the realm of entertainment.

Reed Hastings' entrepreneurial journey exemplifies the transformative power of streaming technology and the impact of disruptive innovation. His vision for Netflix, coupled with his commitment to personalization and original content, has redefined the entertainment landscape and changed the way people consume media around the globe.

As we delve into the remarkable story of Reed Hastings, we witness the triumphs, challenges, and the profound impact he has had on the entertainment industry. Hastings' dedication to technological advancements, his unwavering pursuit of customer satisfaction, and his belief in the power of data and personalization continue to inspire individuals, creators, and businesses to embrace innovation, challenge the status quo, and shape the future of entertainment in an ever-evolving digital era.

21. Marc Benioff

As the co-founder and CEO of Salesforce, Marc Benioff has reshaped the technology industry with his visionary approach to cloud computing and his commitment to philanthropy. His entrepreneurial journey is characterized by a relentless pursuit of customer success, a focus on social impact, and a trailblazing leadership style that has propelled Salesforce to become a global leader in customer relationship management (CRM) software.

Born in San Francisco, California, in 1964, Benioff's early fascination with technology paved the way for his career in the industry. He honed his skills at Oracle Corporation, where he spent 13 years in various leadership roles. It was during his time at Oracle that Benioff recognized the untapped potential of cloud computing and envisioned a new way for businesses to manage their customer relationships.

In 1999, Benioff co-founded Salesforce, a cloud-based CRM software company that disrupted the traditional on-premises software model. Salesforce's innovative approach to delivering software as a service (SaaS) revolutionized the industry, offering businesses the ability to access powerful CRM tools through the internet, without the need for extensive hardware infrastructure.

Under Benioff's leadership, Salesforce experienced rapid growth and became a global leader in the CRM market. Benioff's unwavering focus on customer success, combined with the company's commitment to innovation and user-friendly interfaces, propelled Salesforce to the forefront of enterprise software. The company's cloud-based platform, Salesforce.com, empowered organizations of all sizes to enhance their sales, marketing, and customer service operations.

Beyond Salesforce's success as a business, Benioff's leadership style has been characterized by a deep sense of social responsibility and a commitment to philanthropy. He has championed corporate activism and has been an advocate for various causes, including environmental sustainability, gender equality, and education. Benioff's commitment to creating a positive social impact led to the establishment of the Salesforce Foundation (now known as Salesforce.org), which provides grants, technology, and volunteer support to nonprofit organizations around the world.

Benioff's trailblazing leadership extends beyond his role at Salesforce. He is known for his visionary thinking and his ability to anticipate industry trends. He has been a vocal proponent of the Fourth Industrial Revolution, emphasizing the importance of artificial intelligence, Internet of Things (IoT), and mobile technologies in shaping the future of business and society.

Marc Benioff's entrepreneurial journey exemplifies the transformative power of cloud computing and the importance of purpose-driven leadership. His vision for Salesforce, coupled with his unwavering commitment to customer success and social impact, has revolutionized the way businesses engage with their customers and has inspired a new generation of leaders to embrace innovation and social responsibility.

As we explore the remarkable story of Marc Benioff, we witness the triumphs, challenges, and the profound impact he has had on the technology industry and beyond. Benioff's dedication to customer-centricity, his trailblazing leadership style, and his belief in the power of business as a platform for positive change continue to inspire entrepreneurs, business leaders, and philanthropists to reimagine the role of technology in driving innovation and making a meaningful difference in the world.

22. Daniel Ek

As the co-founder and CEO of Spotify, Daniel Ek has transformed the way people around the world access and enjoy music. His entrepreneurial journey is characterized by a passion for technology, a deep understanding of user experience, and a vision to create a platform that empowers both artists and listeners.

Born in Stockholm, Sweden, in 1983, Ek showed an early aptitude for technology and entrepreneurship. At the age of 14, he started his first business, a web hosting company. This early experience laid the foundation for his future endeavors and ignited his passion for leveraging technology to reshape industries.

In 2006, Ek co-founded Spotify, a digital music streaming platform that would disrupt the traditional music industry. Ek envisioned a platform that would provide users with access to a vast library of music, anytime and anywhere, while also providing artists with fair compensation for their work. With this vision, Spotify emerged as a pioneer in the music streaming space.

Under Ek's leadership, Spotify revolutionized the way people consume music. The platform's freemium model, offering both free and premium subscription options, made music more accessible to a wider audience. By leveraging technology and algorithms, Spotify personalized the music discovery experience, tailoring recommendations to individual tastes and preferences.

One of Ek's key achievements was forging partnerships with major record labels and independent artists, ensuring a diverse and comprehensive music catalog on the platform. This collaborative approach helped reshape the music industry's business model and led to a resurgence in the popularity of streaming as a primary method of music consumption.

Ek's commitment to empowering artists and supporting their creative journeys has been a driving force behind Spotify's success. Through features like Spotify for Artists and the Spotify Creator Fund, Ek has provided tools and resources to help artists connect with their fans, gain insights into their audience, and monetize their work. This emphasis on artist support has contributed to Spotify's reputation as a platform that champions the interests of both artists and listeners.

Beyond his role at Spotify, Ek has been an advocate for innovation and entrepreneurship. He has invested in and mentored numerous startups, sharing his experiences and insights to support the next generation of entrepreneurs. Ek's belief in the power of technology to transform industries and improve people's lives has made him a respected figure in the global tech community.

Daniel Ek's entrepreneurial journey exemplifies the transformative power of music streaming and the importance of creating a sustainable ecosystem that benefits artists and listeners alike. His vision for Spotify, coupled with his dedication to user experience and artist empowerment, has reshaped the music industry and set new standards for how music is consumed and shared.

As we delve into the remarkable story of Daniel Ek, we witness the triumphs, challenges, and the profound impact he has had on the music industry. Ek's dedication to technology, his commitment to artist support, and his belief in the democratization of music continue to inspire individuals, artists, and music enthusiasts to embrace innovation, reimagine traditional models, and shape the future of music in a digital age.

23. Stewart Butterfield

As the co-founder and CEO of Slack, Stewart Butterfield has redefined how teams and organizations collaborate, communicate, and share information. His entrepreneurial journey is marked by a deep understanding of user experience, a passion for creating inclusive communities, and a vision to revolutionize the way people work together.

Born in Lund, Canada, in 1973, Butterfield displayed a natural talent for problem-solving and design from an early age. He studied philosophy at the University of Victoria and pursued a master's degree in philosophy at the University of Cambridge. Butterfield's diverse educational background and his curiosity about human interaction laid the foundation for his future endeavors.

In 2002, Butterfield co-founded Flickr, a pioneering photo-sharing platform that revolutionized online photo sharing and social networking. Flickr's intuitive interface, robust community features, and emphasis on user-generated content made it a global success and showcased Butterfield's ability to create engaging and collaborative online experiences.

Following the sale of Flickr to Yahoo, Butterfield embarked on a new venture with the creation of Slack in 2013. Slack, a cloud-based collaboration hub, aimed to streamline communication and facilitate teamwork within organizations. Butterfield envisioned a platform that would bring together conversations, files, and tools in one place, enabling teams to work more efficiently and effectively.

Under Butterfield's leadership, Slack quickly gained popularity and became a staple in workplaces worldwide. The platform's intuitive interface, seamless integrations with various productivity tools, and emphasis on real-time communication transformed the way teams collaborate and share information. Slack's threaded conversations, channels, and search capabilities enhanced productivity, fostered transparency, and encouraged a sense of community within organizations.

Butterfield's commitment to inclusivity and diversity has been a driving force behind Slack's success. He has championed diversity and equality in the workplace and has been vocal about the importance of creating an inclusive culture. Butterfield's leadership in promoting workplace diversity has made Slack a platform that values different perspectives and encourages collaboration among individuals from various backgrounds and experiences.

Beyond his role at Slack, Butterfield has been an advocate for entrepreneurship and has mentored aspiring founders and startups. He has shared his insights and experiences, encouraging others to pursue their entrepreneurial dreams and create innovative solutions to societal challenges. Butterfield's belief in the power of collaboration and his passion for building supportive communities continue to inspire individuals and organizations to embrace new ways of working and communicating.

Stewart Butterfield's entrepreneurial journey exemplifies the transformative power of collaboration technology and the importance of fostering inclusive communities. His vision for Slack, coupled with his commitment to user experience and workplace diversity, has reshaped the way teams collaborate, communicate, and share knowledge.

As we delve into the remarkable story of Stewart Butterfield, we witness the triumphs, challenges, and the profound impact he has had on the way people work together. Butterfield's dedication to creating user-friendly platforms, his emphasis on inclusivity, and his belief in the power of collaboration continue to inspire individuals, teams, and organizations to embrace innovative tools, bridge communication gaps, and unlock their full potential in an increasingly interconnected world.

24. Nathan Blecharczyk

Nathan Blecharczyk: is a name synonymous with the sharing economy. As the co-founder and Chief Strategy Officer of Airbnb, Blecharczyk has transformed the way people travel and experience hospitality. His entrepreneurial journey is characterized by a deep understanding of technology, a focus on user experience, and a vision to create a platform that connects travelers with unique accommodations around the world.

Born in Boston, Massachusetts, in 1983, Blecharczyk's passion for technology and problem-solving led him to pursue studies in computer science at Harvard University. While still a student, he co-founded a company called "AgentArts," which developed a music recommendation system. This early entrepreneurial experience set the stage for his future endeavors and ignited his interest in creating innovative solutions to real-world problems.

In 2008, Blecharczyk joined forces with Brian Chesky and Joe Gebbia to co-found Airbnb, an online marketplace for people to rent out their homes or spare rooms to travelers. The idea for Airbnb was born out of a necessity to make ends meet and leverage existing resources during a time of financial need. Blecharczyk's technical expertise and analytical mindset played a vital role in building the platform's infrastructure and ensuring a seamless user experience.

Under Blecharczyk's leadership, Airbnb disrupted the traditional hospitality industry and redefined the concept of travel accommodation. The platform's unique value proposition allowed travelers to experience destinations from a local perspective, fostering cultural exchange and creating memorable experiences. By providing access to a wide range of accommodations, from cozy apartments to luxurious villas, Airbnb empowered both hosts and guests to participate in the sharing economy and form meaningful connections.

Blecharczyk's commitment to safety and trust has been instrumental in Airbnb's success. He played a crucial role in implementing rigorous safety protocols, including guest verification, secure payment systems, and host screening. By prioritizing the well-being of both hosts and guests, Blecharczyk instilled confidence in the Airbnb community, enabling the platform to gain widespread adoption and global recognition.

Beyond his role at Airbnb, Blecharczyk has been an advocate for sustainable travel and community engagement. He has supported initiatives that promote responsible tourism, environmental conservation, and local economic development. Blecharczyk's belief in the power of travel to foster understanding and create positive social impact has shaped Airbnb's commitment to sustainable and ethical practices.

Nathan Blecharczyk's entrepreneurial journey exemplifies the transformative power of the sharing economy and the importance of creating meaningful connections through travel. His vision for Airbnb, coupled with his dedication to user experience and safety, has redefined the way people explore the world, connect with others, and experience hospitality.

As we explore the remarkable story of Nathan Blecharczyk, we witness the triumphs, challenges, and the profound impact he has had on the travel industry. Blecharczyk's dedication to technological innovation, his emphasis on safety and trust, and his belief in the power of sharing resources continue to inspire individuals, hosts, and travelers to embrace the sharing economy, redefine traditional models, and create a more connected and inclusive world through travel.

25. Garret Camp

Garret Camp transformed the transportation industry forever. As the co-founder of Uber, Camp has reshaped the way people move around cities and has created a global phenomenon that has disrupted traditional taxi services. His entrepreneurial journey is characterized by a keen eye for identifying market gaps, a relentless pursuit of efficiency, and a vision to revolutionize urban transportation.

Born in Calgary, Canada, in 1978, Camp demonstrated an early interest in technology and computer programming. He studied electrical engineering and computer science at the University of Calgary, where he developed a solid foundation in technology and entrepreneurship. Camp's natural inclination for problem-solving and his passion for creating impactful solutions laid the groundwork for his future ventures.

In 2009, Camp, along with Travis Kalanick, co-founded Uber, a ride-hailing platform that connects riders with drivers through a mobile app. The idea for Uber emerged from Camp's personal frustration with the existing taxi services and his vision to create a more efficient, convenient, and accessible transportation option. Camp's technological expertise and focus on user experience played a crucial role in designing and developing the Uber platform.

Under Camp's leadership, Uber revolutionized the way people commute and navigate cities. The platform's seamless app interface, real-time GPS tracking, and cashless payment system streamlined the booking and ride experience. Uber's disruptive business model enabled anyone with a car and a smartphone to become a driver, providing new income opportunities and transforming the concept of part-time employment.

Camp's commitment to innovation and expansion has been instrumental in Uber's growth. He played a pivotal role in the company's global expansion, driving Uber's entry into new markets and forging partnerships with local transportation providers. Camp's strategic vision helped Uber become a dominant player in the ride-hailing industry, disrupting traditional taxi services and shaping the future of urban mobility.

Beyond his role at Uber, Camp has been an advocate for sustainable transportation and has invested in various environmentally friendly initiatives. He has supported the development of electric vehicle technologies and explored opportunities to reduce congestion and emissions in urban areas. Camp's belief in the importance of responsible and sustainable transportation has influenced Uber's commitment to environmental sustainability.

Garret Camp's entrepreneurial journey exemplifies the transformative power of technology and the importance of identifying market gaps. His vision for Uber, coupled with his dedication to user experience and efficiency, has revolutionized the way people travel within cities and has created a new paradigm for urban transportation.

As we delve into the remarkable story of Garret Camp, we witness the triumphs, challenges, and the profound impact he has had on the transportation industry. Camp's dedication to technological innovation, his emphasis on user-centric design, and his belief in the power of accessible and efficient transportation continue to inspire entrepreneurs, disrupt traditional industries, and reshape the way people navigate and connect within cities.

26. Andrew Mason

As the co-founder and former CEO of Groupon, Andrew Mason has revolutionized the way people discover and engage with local businesses. His entrepreneurial journey is characterized by a unique approach to collective buying, a passion for innovation, and a vision to connect consumers with local merchants.

Born in Pittsburgh, Pennsylvania, in 1980, Mason showed an early interest in music and technology. He studied music at Northwestern University and later pursued a career as a software developer. Mason's diverse background in music, technology, and entrepreneurship provided him with a unique perspective and a creative mindset.

In 2008, Mason founded The Point, a social activism platform that allowed users to organize and participate in collective actions. It was during this time that Mason recognized the potential of collective buying to connect consumers with local businesses and create mutually beneficial opportunities. This realization led to the birth of Groupon, a platform that offers daily deals and discounts on products, services, and experiences.

Under Mason's leadership, Groupon experienced rapid growth and became a global phenomenon. The platform's innovative approach to group buying and its ability to leverage the power of collective purchasing attracted millions of subscribers and established Groupon as a dominant player in the local commerce space. Mason's creative marketing campaigns, including quirky and humorous emails, helped Groupon gain widespread attention and popularity.

Mason's commitment to supporting local businesses has been a driving force behind Groupon's success. By partnering with small and medium-sized businesses, Groupon provided them with a platform to attract new customers, increase visibility, and boost sales. This symbiotic relationship between Groupon and local merchants fostered economic growth and revitalized communities.

Beyond his role at Groupon, Mason has continued to pursue innovative ventures and invest in technology startups. His curiosity and entrepreneurial spirit have led him to explore new industries and contribute to the development of disruptive business models. Mason's passion for creativity and his ability to identify emerging trends have made him a respected figure in the startup community.

Andrew Mason's entrepreneurial journey exemplifies the transformative power of collective buying and the importance of connecting consumers with local businesses. His vision for Groupon, coupled with his creative marketing strategies and commitment to supporting local commerce, has reshaped the way people discover, experience, and engage with businesses in their communities.

As we delve into the remarkable story of Andrew Mason, we witness the triumphs, challenges, and the profound impact he has had on the local commerce landscape. Mason's dedication to innovation, his emphasis on community engagement, and his belief in the power of collective action continue to inspire entrepreneurs, encourage consumer exploration, and shape the future of local commerce in a digital age.

27. Aaron Levie

As the co-founder and CEO of Box, Aaron Levie has redefined how businesses store, manage, and share their digital content. His entrepreneurial journey is marked by a relentless pursuit of simplicity, a commitment to user-centric design, and a vision to empower organizations through seamless collaboration.

Born in Los Altos, California, in 1985, Levie demonstrated an entrepreneurial spirit from a young age. While still in high school, he recognized the potential of cloud storage and saw the need for a secure and accessible platform for businesses to store and share their files. This realization laid the foundation for his future venture, Box.

In 2005, Levie co-founded Box, a cloud-based content management and collaboration platform. With its user-friendly interface, robust security measures, and seamless integration with other productivity tools, Box quickly gained traction among businesses of all sizes. Levie's passion for simplifying complex workflows and his relentless focus on user experience played a pivotal role in shaping the platform's success.

Under Levie's leadership, Box has become a global leader in cloud content management, serving millions of users and enabling organizations to securely store, organize, and collaborate on their digital assets. Box's platform offers a centralized hub for businesses to store files, collaborate in real-time, and streamline workflows across teams and departments. Levie's vision for seamless collaboration has transformed the way organizations work, breaking down silos and fostering productivity and innovation.

Levie's commitment to security and data privacy has been instrumental in establishing Box as a trusted platform for sensitive business information. He has continuously emphasized the importance of maintaining strict security protocols, encryption, and compliance standards to protect user data. Levie's proactive approach to security has earned the trust of enterprises and has positioned Box as a leader in secure cloud storage solutions.

Beyond his role at Box, Levie is known for his thought leadership and advocacy for digital transformation in the enterprise. He has been a vocal proponent of cloud computing, collaboration, and the need for organizations to adapt to the rapidly evolving digital landscape. Levie's insights and commentary on technology trends have made him a respected figure in the industry and a sought-after speaker at conferences and events.

Aaron Levie's entrepreneurial journey exemplifies the transformative power of cloud storage and collaboration and the importance of user-centric design. His vision for Box, coupled with his dedication to simplicity and security, has revolutionized the way businesses store, access, and collaborate on their digital content.

As we explore the remarkable story of Aaron Levie, we witness the triumphs, challenges, and the profound impact he has had on the enterprise technology landscape. Levie's dedication to innovation, his emphasis on user experience, and his belief in the power of seamless collaboration continue to inspire organizations, drive digital transformation, and reshape the future of work in an increasingly interconnected world.

28. Hiroshi Mikitani

As the founder and CEO of Rakuten, Hiroshi Mikitani has reshaped the way people shop online and has built a global empire of e-commerce services. His entrepreneurial journey is characterized by a relentless pursuit of customer-centricity, a passion for innovation, and a vision to create a comprehensive online marketplace.

Born in Kobe, Japan, in 1965, Mikitani developed a keen interest in business and technology from an early age. He studied at Hitotsubashi University, where he gained a solid foundation in economics and business management. Mikitani's entrepreneurial spirit led him to found his first company, Future Systems Inc., which provided software solutions for businesses.

In 1997, Mikitani founded Rakuten, an online marketplace that aimed to connect consumers with a wide range of products and services. Initially focused on the Japanese market, Rakuten quickly expanded its offerings, diversifying into various sectors such as e-commerce, travel, finance, and digital content. Mikitani's vision for Rakuten was to create a one-stop platform that catered to the diverse needs of consumers and businesses alike.

Under Mikitani's leadership, Rakuten experienced rapid growth and became a global e-commerce powerhouse. The platform's user-friendly interface, extensive product offerings, and unique loyalty program, Rakuten Super Points, attracted millions of users and established Rakuten as a trusted brand in the e-commerce industry. Mikitani's commitment to providing exceptional customer experiences and fostering strong relationships with merchants propelled Rakuten's success.

Mikitani's emphasis on innovation and technology has been a driving force behind Rakuten's evolution. He led the company's expansion into various sectors, acquiring and investing in technology-driven companies to enhance Rakuten's ecosystem. Additionally, Mikitani championed the development of Rakuten's own payment system, Rakuten Pay, and the integration of artificial intelligence and data analytics to personalize the shopping experience for customers.

Beyond his role at Rakuten, Mikitani has been a strong advocate for economic empowerment and entrepreneurship. He has supported initiatives that foster innovation and nurture startup ecosystems, both in Japan and globally. Mikitani's commitment to social impact has led him to establish the Rakuten Social Accelerator, a program that supports social entrepreneurs tackling critical issues around the world.

Hiroshi Mikitani's entrepreneurial journey exemplifies the transformative power of e-commerce and the importance of customer-centricity. His vision for Rakuten, coupled with his dedication to innovation and technology, has revolutionized the way people shop and engage with online marketplaces.

As we delve into the remarkable story of Hiroshi Mikitani, we witness the triumphs, challenges, and the profound impact he has had on the e-commerce landscape. Mikitani's dedication to customer satisfaction, his emphasis on innovation, and his belief in the power of digital marketplaces continue to inspire entrepreneurs, drive economic growth, and shape the future of online commerce in an increasingly interconnected world.

29. Anthony Tan

As the co-founder and CEO of Grab, Anthony Tan has revolutionized the way people move around cities and has created a super app that offers a wide range of services. His entrepreneurial journey is marked by a relentless drive for excellence, a commitment to solving local challenges, and a vision to improve the lives of millions in the region.

Born and raised in Malaysia, Tan hails from a family with a background in the automotive industry. He pursued his education at Harvard Business School, where he gained valuable insights into entrepreneurship and leadership. Tan's exposure to the vibrant startup ecosystem in the United States sparked his ambition to make a significant impact in his home region.

In 2012, Tan co-founded Grab, initially known as MyTeksi, with the aim of addressing the transportation challenges faced by people in Southeast Asia. Grab started as a ride-hailing platform, connecting passengers with drivers through a mobile app, but quickly expanded its services to include food delivery, parcel delivery, financial services, and more. Tan's vision was to create a comprehensive super app that catered to the diverse needs of the Southeast Asian population.

Under Tan's leadership, Grab has become a dominant force in the region's transportation industry. The platform's commitment to safety, reliability, and convenience has resonated with millions of users across Southeast Asia. Tan's focus on localized solutions, including cash payments and tailored services for specific markets, has played a crucial role in Grab's rapid growth and market dominance.

Beyond transportation, Tan has been instrumental in leveraging Grab's platform to provide essential services and promote financial inclusion in Southeast Asia. GrabPay, the company's digital wallet, enables millions of users to access financial services, make cashless payments, and participate in the digital economy. Tan's commitment to creating a more inclusive and sustainable future has driven Grab's expansion into areas such as renewable energy and micro-lending.

Tan's entrepreneurial spirit and dedication to social impact have garnered recognition and accolades. He has been recognized as one of Fortune's "40 Under 40" and Forbes' "30 Under 30" lists, among other honors. Tan's vision and leadership have also inspired the next generation of entrepreneurs in Southeast Asia, fostering a vibrant startup ecosystem in the region.

Anthony Tan's entrepreneurial journey exemplifies the transformative power of technology and the importance of addressing local challenges. His vision for Grab, coupled with his unwavering commitment to safety, convenience, and financial inclusion, has revolutionized the way people in Southeast Asia commute, access essential services, and participate in the digital economy.

As we delve into the remarkable story of Anthony Tan, we witness the triumphs, challenges, and the profound impact he has had on the transportation landscape in Southeast Asia. Tan's dedication to innovation, his focus on localized solutions, and his belief in the power of technology to improve lives continue to inspire entrepreneurs, reshape industries, and drive social and economic progress in the region.

30. Jensen Huang

Jensen Huang: a name synonymous with innovation, technological advancement, and the transformation of graphics technology. As the co-founder and CEO of NVIDIA, Huang has spearheaded the development of cutting-edge GPUs (Graphics Processing Units) that have revolutionized industries and fueled the rise of artificial intelligence. His entrepreneurial journey is characterized by a relentless pursuit of excellence, a passion for pushing the boundaries of what's possible, and a vision to empower industries with accelerated computing.

Born in Tainan, Taiwan, in 1963, Huang moved to the United States at a young age to pursue his education. He earned his bachelor's degree in electrical engineering from Oregon State University and later pursued a master's degree from Stanford University. Huang's early career included working at companies like LSI Logic and Advanced Micro Devices (AMD), where he honed his expertise in graphics technology.

In 1993, Huang co-founded NVIDIA, initially focusing on designing high-performance graphics processors for the gaming industry. Under his leadership, NVIDIA quickly gained recognition for its innovative GPU architecture and its commitment to delivering superior graphics performance. Huang's vision went beyond gaming, as he saw the potential for GPUs to revolutionize other industries such as data centers, artificial intelligence, and autonomous vehicles.

NVIDIA's GPUs have become the gold standard in graphics processing, enabling stunning visual experiences in video games, virtual reality, and professional graphics applications. Under Huang's guidance, NVIDIA expanded its product portfolio to cater to the diverse needs of industries requiring high-performance computing. This led to the development of CUDA, a parallel computing platform and programming model, and the creation of specialized GPUs for applications in data centers, scientific research, and AI training and inference.

Huang's leadership and foresight have positioned NVIDIA as a global technology powerhouse. The company's GPUs have become essential components in industries such as AI, deep learning, autonomous vehicles, and high-performance computing. NVIDIA's dedication to innovation and its focus on delivering breakthrough technologies have earned it numerous awards and accolades, solidifying its reputation as a leading player in the semiconductor industry.

Beyond his role at NVIDIA, Huang is known for his charismatic presence and his ability to inspire and motivate. He has a passion for sharing his knowledge and insights, often delivering captivating keynote speeches at industry events. Huang's vision extends to fostering collaboration and partnerships with other technology companies, enabling NVIDIA to expand its influence and drive advancements in various fields.

Jensen Huang's entrepreneurial journey exemplifies the transformative power of graphics technology and the importance of pushing the boundaries of innovation. His vision for NVIDIA, coupled with his dedication to excellence and his belief in the potential of GPUs, has revolutionized industries, empowered researchers, and accelerated the pace of technological advancement.

As we explore the remarkable story of Jensen Huang, we witness the triumphs, challenges, and the profound impact he has had on the graphics technology landscape. Huang's unwavering commitment to innovation, his relentless pursuit of excellence, and his vision for the future continue to inspire technologists, shape industries, and drive the next wave of technological breakthroughs in a rapidly evolving digital world.

31. Tony Fadell

Tony Fadell is a name that has been inextricably linked to the concepts of creativity and design, as well as the revolution in consumer electronics. As the co-founder of Nest and one of the key minds behind the iPod, Fadell has reimagined everyday devices, shaping the way people interact with technology. His entrepreneurial journey is characterized by a deep passion for elegant design, a commitment to user-centered experiences, and a vision to create intuitive and intelligent products.

Born in Detroit, Michigan, in 1969, Fadell displayed a natural curiosity for technology from an early age. He pursued his passion by studying computer engineering at the University of Michigan. Fadell's career path led him to work at General Magic, a pioneering company in the realm of handheld devices, where he gained valuable experience in product development and innovation.

In 2001, Fadell joined Apple and played a pivotal role in the creation of the iPod, a portable music player that revolutionized the way people listen to music. Fadell's expertise in hardware design, coupled with his keen understanding of consumer needs, contributed to the development of the iconic device. The iPod's sleek design, simple user interface, and integration with iTunes reshaped the music industry and propelled Apple's success in the consumer electronics market.

Building upon the success of the iPod, Fadell went on to co-found Nest Labs in 2010. Nest's mission was to transform mundane household devices into smart, connected, and energy-efficient appliances. The company's flagship product, the Nest Learning Thermostat, brought intuitive temperature control to homes, learning users' preferences and optimizing energy usage. Fadell's vision for creating devices that seamlessly blend technology with everyday life resonated with consumers, and Nest quickly gained recognition as a leader in the smart home industry.

Under Fadell's leadership, Nest expanded its product line to include security cameras, video doorbells, and smoke detectors, all interconnected and controllable through a unified platform. Fadell's emphasis on user-centered design and the integration of artificial intelligence and machine learning set Nest apart, offering homeowners a more intuitive and personalized experience.

In 2014, Google acquired Nest Labs, recognizing Fadell's talent for innovation and his ability to create groundbreaking products. Fadell continued to lead Nest within Google and contributed to the development of Google's broader smart home ecosystem.

Beyond his work at Nest, Fadell is known for his commitment to sustainability and environmental conservation. He has advocated for energy-efficient technologies and has emphasized the importance of reducing energy consumption through smart home devices.

Tony Fadell's entrepreneurial journey exemplifies the transformative power of consumer electronics and the importance of user-centered design. His vision for creating intuitive and intelligent devices, coupled with his expertise in hardware and software integration, has revolutionized industries and shaped the way people interact with technology in their everyday lives.

As we delve into the remarkable story of Tony Fadell, we witness the triumphs, challenges, and the profound impact he has had on the consumer electronics landscape. Fadell's dedication to innovation, his unwavering commitment to elegant design, and his vision for seamless integration continue to inspire technologists, designers, and entrepreneurs, driving the next wave of breakthroughs in the rapidly evolving world of consumer technology.

32. Brian Acton

As the co-founder of one of the world's most popular messaging apps, Brian Acton has transformed the way people connect and communicate across the globe. His entrepreneurial journey is marked by perseverance, a commitment to privacy, and a vision to provide a simple and secure messaging platform for millions of users.

Born in Michigan, United States, in 1972, Acton developed a passion for technology from a young age. He studied computer science at Stanford University and began his career working in prominent technology companies like Apple and Yahoo. It was during his tenure at Yahoo that Acton crossed paths with Jan Koum, and together, they laid the foundation for a revolutionary messaging platform.

In 2009, Acton and Koum co-founded WhatsApp, a messaging app that aimed to provide a seamless and reliable communication experience. At its core, WhatsApp prioritized simplicity, speed, and privacy, allowing users to send text messages, voice messages, images, and videos with ease. Acton and Koum's commitment to providing an ad-free and data-secure platform resonated with users worldwide.

Under Acton's leadership as a co-founder and executive,

WhatsApp experienced exponential growth, attracting millions of users and gaining popularity for its user-friendly interface and strong encryption protocols. The app became a crucial tool for personal and business communication, transcending geographical boundaries and language barriers.

In 2014, Facebook acquired WhatsApp, recognizing the immense value and potential of the platform. Acton remained with WhatsApp for a few years after the acquisition before departing to pursue other ventures. However, his influence on WhatsApp's trajectory and the emphasis on user privacy remained ingrained in the app's DNA.

Acton's entrepreneurial journey didn't end with WhatsApp. He became a vocal advocate for digital privacy and took on new ventures to champion this cause. In 2018, Acton co-founded the Signal Foundation, a non-profit organization that supports the development of the Signal messaging app, known for its strong encryption and commitment to user privacy. Acton's dedication to protecting user data and preserving privacy rights continues to shape the conversation surrounding technology and communication.

Brian Acton's entrepreneurial journey embodies the power of innovation and the significance of secure communication in the digital age. His vision for WhatsApp, coupled with his unwavering commitment to user privacy, has transformed the way people connect and exchange messages globally.

As we explore the remarkable story of Brian Acton, we witness the triumphs, challenges, and the profound impact he has had on the communication landscape. Acton's dedication to simplicity, security, and privacy continues to inspire entrepreneurs, shape the future of messaging apps, and advocate for a digital world where users' personal information is safeguarded.

33. David Karp

David Karp spurred the world forward in the realm of creativity, blogging, and the creation of Tumblr. As the founder of one of the most influential microblogging platforms, Karp has revolutionized the way people express themselves and share content online. His entrepreneurial journey is characterized by a passion for user-generated content, a commitment to simplicity, and a vision to empower individuals to build their online communities.

Born and raised in New York City, Karp demonstrated a keen interest in technology from an early age. He dropped out of high school at the age of 15 to pursue his passion for programming and web development. Karp's talent and entrepreneurial spirit caught the attention of established industry figures, leading to various consulting and freelance opportunities.

In 2007, at the age of 21, Karp founded Tumblr. The platform aimed to provide a simple, intuitive, and visually appealing space for users to share their thoughts, ideas, and creative content. Tumblr's unique blend of blogging and social networking quickly gained traction, attracting millions of users who embraced its user-friendly interface and customization options.

Under Karp's leadership, Tumblr became a hub for creative expression, allowing users to share text posts, photos, quotes, links, audio, and videos. The platform's emphasis on multimedia content and its reblogging feature encouraged collaboration and community building. Tumblr fostered a vibrant community of artists, writers, photographers, and creators who used the platform as a canvas to showcase their work and connect with like-minded individuals.

Tumblr's impact on popular culture and internet communities cannot be overstated. It played a significant role in shaping meme culture, supporting social justice movements, and providing a platform for marginalized voices to be heard. Karp's commitment to free expression and enabling individuals to find their creative voice made Tumblr a powerful medium for self-expression and cultural exchange.

In 2013, Yahoo acquired Tumblr, recognizing its influence and potential. Karp continued to lead the platform as CEO for several years, maintaining its unique identity and fostering a supportive environment for users. While his tenure at Tumblr had its challenges, Karp remained an influential figure in the tech and creative industries.

David Karp's entrepreneurial journey exemplifies the power of user-generated content and the importance of platforms that empower individuals to express themselves. His vision for Tumblr, coupled with his commitment to simplicity and fostering creative communities, transformed the landscape of online expression and community building.

As we delve into the remarkable story of David Karp, we witness the triumphs, challenges, and the profound impact he has had on the blogging and social networking landscape. Karp's dedication to empowering creativity, amplifying diverse voices, and fostering a sense of belonging continues to inspire creators, shape online communities, and pave the way for new forms of digital expression in a rapidly evolving digital era.

34. Palmer Luckey

Palmer Luckey is the founder of of Oculus and a pioneer in the world of Virtual Reality (VR). As the creator of the Oculus Rift, Luckey played a pivotal role in bringing immersive VR experiences to the masses. His entrepreneurial journey is characterized by a passion for virtual reality, a dedication to pushing the boundaries of technology, and a vision to revolutionize the way people interact with digital content.

Born in Long Beach, California, in 1992, Luckey developed a fascination with virtual reality and 3D graphics at a young age. As a teenager, he began tinkering with various virtual reality headsets, experimenting with different designs and technologies. Luckey's innovative spirit and expertise in hardware development and programming set the foundation for what would become a groundbreaking invention.

In 2012, at the age of 19, Luckey founded Oculus VR and launched a Kickstarter campaign for the Oculus Rift, a high-quality virtual reality headset. The campaign was a resounding success, raising millions of dollars and garnering immense interest from developers and enthusiasts alike. Luckey's determination to create an affordable and accessible VR device captured the attention of the technology industry.

The success of the Kickstarter campaign caught the eye of tech veteran Brendan Iribe, who joined Oculus VR as CEO. Together, Luckey and Iribe worked to refine and improve the Oculus Rift, turning it into a more polished and immersive virtual reality experience.

In 2014, Facebook acquired Oculus VR, recognizing the transformative potential of virtual reality technology. The acquisition provided Oculus with the resources needed to accelerate the development of the Oculus Rift and further expand its capabilities. Luckey continued to work on VR technology within Facebook, contributing to the development of subsequent Oculus headsets and supporting the growth of the virtual reality ecosystem.

Palmer Luckey's vision for virtual reality extended beyond gaming and entertainment. He saw the potential of VR as a tool for education, training, social interaction, and even therapy. His commitment to creating an open platform for developers to build VR experiences opened the door for a wide range of applications, from gaming to medical simulations and architectural visualization.

Despite leaving Facebook in 2017, Luckey's influence on the virtual reality industry remains profound. He has continued to explore new technologies, advocate for open platforms, and support developers in their efforts to create transformative VR experiences.

Palmer Luckey's entrepreneurial journey exemplifies the power of passion, innovation, and vision in shaping transformative technologies. His work with Oculus has played a key role in popularizing virtual reality and inspiring a new generation of technologists to explore the possibilities of immersive digital experiences.

As we explore the remarkable story of Palmer Luckey, we witness the triumphs, challenges, and the profound impact he has had on the virtual reality landscape. Luckey's dedication to pushing the boundaries of technology, coupled with his commitment to accessibility and openness, continues to inspire creators, developers, and enthusiasts to explore the exciting possibilities that lie ahead in the ever-evolving world of virtual reality.

35. Elizabeth Holmes

Elizabeth Holmes: a name that once evoked admiration and awe in the world of entrepreneurship, only to become synonymous with scandal and deception. As the founder and former CEO of Theranos, Holmes captured the attention of the tech industry and the public with her ambitious vision of revolutionizing healthcare through groundbreaking blood-testing technology. However, her entrepreneurial journey took a dramatic turn, ultimately leading to her downfall.

Born in Washington, D.C., in 1984, Holmes showed early signs of ambition and determination. She attended Stanford University, studying chemical engineering and immersing herself in the world of biotechnology. It was during her time at Stanford that the seeds of her future venture, Theranos, began to take shape.

In 2003, at the age of 19, Holmes dropped out of Stanford to start Theranos. The company aimed to develop a revolutionary blood-testing device that could perform a wide range of diagnostic tests with just a few drops of blood, promising faster results, lower costs, and increased accessibility. Holmes presented herself as a visionary and became a prominent figure in the healthcare and technology industries.

However, as the years passed, questions began to emerge about the efficacy and accuracy of Theranos' technology. Investigations and scrutiny revealed that the company had misled investors, medical professionals, and the public about the capabilities of its blood-testing device. The technology that had been hailed as a game-changer was revealed to be flawed and unreliable.

The revelations surrounding Theranos led to a cascade of legal and regulatory challenges. Holmes and former Theranos president Ramesh "Sunny" Balwani faced charges of fraud, with allegations of misleading investors, doctors, and patients. The downfall of Theranos served as a cautionary tale about the importance of transparency, integrity, and ethical practices in the world of entrepreneurship.

Elizabeth Holmes' story serves as a reminder of the dangers of unchecked ambition and the consequences of placing success above ethics and accountability. Her rise and fall have ignited conversations about corporate governance, regulatory oversight, and the responsibility of entrepreneurs to prioritize the well-being of consumers and society at large.

As we examine the remarkable story of Elizabeth Holmes, we witness the highs and lows, the allure and the deception, and the profound impact she had on the perception of entrepreneurship in the healthcare industry. Holmes' story serves as a reminder that trust and integrity are the bedrocks of any successful venture, and the consequences of breaching that trust can be severe.

While Elizabeth Holmes' journey may have ended in controversy and legal battles, her story remains a cautionary tale that has sparked important discussions about ethics, accountability, and the need for transparency in the pursuit of transformative innovation.

36. Ben Horowitz

As a renowned investor, entrepreneur, and author, Ben Horowitz has played a pivotal role in shaping the startup ecosystem and supporting the growth of countless innovative companies. His journey is characterized by a deep understanding of the challenges faced by entrepreneurs and a commitment to empowering them to succeed.

Born in London, England, in 1966, Horowitz developed a passion for technology and business from a young age. He attended Columbia University, where he studied computer science and became immersed in the world of software development. After graduation, Horowitz embarked on an entrepreneurial journey, co-founding several tech companies, including Loudcloud and Opsware.

The experience of building and leading these companies gave Horowitz invaluable insights into the struggles and triumphs of entrepreneurship. After the successful acquisition of Opsware by Hewlett-Packard in 2007, Horowitz turned his attention to venture capital, recognizing the opportunity to support and mentor the next generation of entrepreneurs.

In 2009, Horowitz, along with Marc Andreessen, co-founded Andreessen Horowitz (often referred to as a16z), a prominent venture capital firm known for its investments in technology startups. The firm quickly gained a reputation for its hands-on approach, deep industry expertise, and commitment to providing more than just financial backing. Horowitz played a crucial role in shaping the firm's culture and guiding its investments, focusing on sectors such as software, enterprise technology, and internet infrastructure.

Beyond his work as a venture capitalist, Horowitz is also a prolific writer and author. In his book "The Hard Thing About Hard Things," he shares candid insights and practical advice on navigating the challenges of building and scaling a company. His writings have become a valuable resource for entrepreneurs and leaders, offering guidance on topics ranging from organizational culture to decision-making in high-stakes situations.

Ben Horowitz's entrepreneurial journey has been marked by his ability to bridge the gap between investor and entrepreneur. His deep empathy for the struggles faced by founders, coupled with his strategic mindset and industry knowledge, has made him a trusted advisor and mentor to many. He continues to be actively involved in the startup community, serving on boards and providing guidance to entrepreneurs at various stages of their journey.

As we delve into the remarkable story of Ben Horowitz, we witness his unwavering commitment to nurturing entrepreneurial spirit and fostering innovation. Horowitz's influence on the startup ecosystem extends beyond financial investments, as he empowers entrepreneurs with the knowledge, support, and resources needed to overcome challenges and build successful companies.

Through his work at Andreessen Horowitz and his writings, Ben Horowitz has become a beacon of inspiration for aspiring entrepreneurs and a guiding force in the world of technology and venture capital. His legacy as an investor, mentor, and thought leader continues to shape the entrepreneurial landscape, driving innovation and fostering the growth of transformative companies.

37. Phil Knight

As the co-founder and former CEO of one of the world's most iconic and influential sportswear brands, Nike, Phil Knight has left an indelible mark on the world of sports, fashion, and entrepreneurship. His journey is characterized by relentless determination, groundbreaking marketing strategies, and a passion for empowering athletes.

Born in Portland, Oregon, in 1938, Knight developed a love for sports and a competitive spirit from an early age. He excelled in track and field during his high school and college years, earning a scholarship to the University of Oregon. It was at university that Knight first came up with the idea of importing high-quality athletic shoes from Japan, sparking the beginning of his entrepreneurial journey.

In 1964, after completing his MBA at Stanford University, Knight co-founded Blue Ribbon Sports (later renamed Nike) with his former track coach, Bill Bowerman. The company started as a distributor for Japanese athletic shoe manufacturer Onitsuka Tiger (now ASICS), importing and selling their shoes in the United States.

Knight's entrepreneurial vision went beyond simply distributing shoes. He recognized the potential to design and market innovative footwear specifically tailored to the needs of athletes. In 1971, Nike introduced its own line of shoes, featuring the now-iconic "Swoosh" logo designed by Carolyn Davidson. The Nike brand quickly gained recognition and popularity among athletes and sports enthusiasts, propelling the company to unprecedented heights.

One of Knight's most significant contributions to Nike's success was his innovative marketing strategies. He understood the power of branding and endorsement deals, forging partnerships with world-renowned athletes like Michael Jordan, Serena Williams, and Tiger Woods. These collaborations not only elevated Nike's image but also solidified its association with high performance and athletic excellence.

Under Knight's leadership, Nike revolutionized the athletic footwear industry through continuous innovation and technological advancements. The company introduced groundbreaking technologies like Air cushioning, Flyknit material, and the Nike+ running system, further solidifying its position as a leader in the sportswear market.

Beyond his role at Nike, Knight has also been recognized for his philanthropic efforts. He and his wife, Penny, have made substantial contributions to education, healthcare, and scientific research. Their commitment to giving back has had a positive impact on numerous communities and causes.

Phil Knight's entrepreneurial journey exemplifies the power of determination, innovation, and a relentless pursuit of excellence. His visionary leadership and unwavering commitment to athletes and their needs have made Nike a global powerhouse, influencing sports culture and inspiring millions around the world.

As we explore the remarkable story of Phil Knight, we witness the triumphs, challenges, and the profound impact he has had on the athletic footwear industry. Knight's entrepreneurial spirit, combined with his focus on innovation, branding, and athlete empowerment, continues to shape the sports landscape and inspire future generations of entrepreneurs to dream big and pursue their passions.

38. Pierre Omidyar

Pierre Omidyar: a name synonymous with online commerce, philanthropy, and the founding of eBay. As a visionary entrepreneur and philanthropist, Omidyar has made a significant impact on the e-commerce industry while leveraging his success to drive positive change in the world. His journey is characterized by a commitment to empowering individuals, fostering economic opportunity, and promoting social good.

Born in Paris, France, in 1967, Omidyar displayed an early interest in technology and entrepreneurship. He studied computer science at Tufts University, where he honed his skills and passion for coding and software development. After graduation, Omidyar worked for various tech companies, gaining valuable experience and insight into the emerging digital landscape.

In 1995, Omidyar launched AuctionWeb, a website that allowed people to buy and sell goods online through an auction format. This platform, which later became known as eBay, quickly gained traction and revolutionized the way individuals conducted commerce. eBay's user-friendly interface, trust-building features, and Omidyar's commitment to customer satisfaction made it a resounding success.

Omidyar's vision for eBay extended beyond just facilitating transactions. He saw the platform as a means to empower individuals, creating economic opportunities for entrepreneurs and small businesses around the world. Through eBay, people could turn their hobbies, collectibles, and unique goods into viable businesses, tapping into a global marketplace.

Under Omidyar's leadership, eBay expanded its reach and diversified its offerings, acquiring companies like PayPal, Half.com, and Skype. These acquisitions further strengthened eBay's position as a leader in online commerce and payment services, providing users with a seamless and secure way to transact online.

Beyond his achievements in the business world, Omidyar is known for his philanthropic endeavors. In 2004, he and his wife, Pam, established the Omidyar Network, a philanthropic investment firm that supports initiatives promoting social impact and systemic change. The Omidyar Network focuses on areas such as education, governance, financial inclusion, and technology for social good, aiming to create a more equitable and inclusive society.

Omidyar's philanthropic efforts have extended to various causes and organizations, including investigative journalism through the support of initiatives like The Intercept and First Look Media. His belief in the power of a free press and the importance of holding power accountable has made a significant impact on media and democracy.

Pierre Omidyar's entrepreneurial journey exemplifies the potential of technology to drive positive change and empower individuals. His creation of eBay revolutionized e-commerce, democratizing the marketplace and giving rise to countless entrepreneurs and small businesses. His commitment to philanthropy and social impact has further amplified his influence, channeling his resources and expertise toward making a meaningful difference in society.

As we delve into the remarkable story of Pierre Omidyar, we witness the transformative power of entrepreneurship and the potential to combine business success with philanthropic endeavors.

Omidyar's dedication to empowering individuals and promoting social good continues to inspire a new generation of entrepreneurs and change-makers, encouraging them to create businesses that have a positive impact on people's lives and communities.

39. Richard Branson

As the founder of Virgin Group, Richard Branson has built an empire of diverse businesses spanning industries such as music, airlines, telecommunications, and space travel. His charismatic personality, daring spirit, and relentless pursuit of new frontiers have made him one of the most recognized and admired entrepreneurs of our time.

Born in London, England, in 1950, Branson demonstrated an entrepreneurial spirit from a young age. At the age of 16, he started his first business venture, a student magazine called "Student." This early taste of success fueled his ambition and set the stage for his future endeavors.

In 1970, Branson established Virgin as a mail-order record retailer. The company quickly expanded, opening its first record store in London, and later diversifying into music production with the launch of Virgin Records. Branson's ability to identify emerging trends and his keen eye for talent helped him sign notable artists such as the Rolling Stones, Janet Jackson, and Phil Collins, solidifying Virgin Records as a prominent player in the music industry.

However, Branson's entrepreneurial ambitions didn't stop at music. He ventured into numerous industries, each marked by his distinctive Virgin brand and his willingness to challenge the status quo. Virgin Atlantic Airways took to the skies in 1984, disrupting the airline industry with its innovative approach to customer service and its focus on the customer experience.

Branson's appetite for adventure and pushing boundaries led him to explore new frontiers. In 2004, he founded Virgin Galactic, a spaceflight company aiming to make commercial space travel a reality. Although the journey to achieving this goal has been fraught with challenges and setbacks, Branson's determination to democratize space travel has captured the imagination of millions worldwide.

Beyond his business ventures, Branson is known for his philanthropic efforts and commitment to social causes. The Virgin Group has championed various initiatives focused on environmental sustainability, renewable energy, and social entrepreneurship. Branson's dedication to using his resources and influence to make a positive impact on the world has earned him respect and admiration.

Branson's entrepreneurial journey is not without its failures and setbacks. However, his ability to bounce back from adversity and maintain a fearless, optimistic outlook has become a hallmark of his character. His unconventional approach, boundless energy, and belief in the power of people have made him an inspirational figure for aspiring entrepreneurs.

As we explore the remarkable story of Richard Branson, we witness a man who has continually pushed the boundaries of what is possible. Branson's relentless pursuit of new horizons, his unyielding belief in his vision, and his unwavering commitment to creating extraordinary experiences have shaped his legacy as a maverick entrepreneur and adventurer.

Richard Branson's entrepreneurial journey serves as a reminder to embrace curiosity, take calculated risks, and approach challenges with resilience and optimism. His unwavering commitment to innovation, his determination to make a positive impact, and his zest for life continue to inspire individuals around the world to dream big and pursue their own extraordinary ventures.

40. Michael Dell

As the founder and CEO of Dell Inc., Michael Dell has become known worldwide and is associated with technology through his pioneering vision, customer-centric approach, and relentless pursuit of excellence.

Born in Houston, Texas, in 1965, Michael Dell exhibited an early fascination with computers and technology. At the age of 15, he started selling upgrade kits for personal computers from his dorm room at the University of Texas at Austin. Recognizing the untapped potential of the emerging PC market, Dell dropped out of college to fully devote himself to his business venture.

In 1984, at the age of 19, Dell officially founded Dell Computer Corporation (now Dell Inc.) with a simple yet groundbreaking idea: to sell customized personal computers directly to consumers, cutting out the middleman and offering competitive prices. This direct-to-consumer model not only disrupted the traditional distribution channels of the computer industry but also allowed Dell to provide tailored solutions to meet the specific needs of its customers.

Dell's emphasis on customer experience and customization quickly propelled the company to success. By offering a wide range of customizable computer systems and providing exceptional customer service, Dell became a trusted brand in the industry. The company's commitment to quality and efficiency earned it a reputation for delivering reliable and affordable technology solutions.

Under Michael Dell's leadership, the company expanded its product offerings beyond personal computers to include servers, storage devices, networking equipment, and software solutions. This diversification strategy enabled Dell to cater to the evolving needs of businesses and consumers alike, solidifying its position as a leading technology provider.

In 2004, Dell stepped down as CEO but continued to be involved in shaping the company's direction as Chairman of the Board. During his absence from the CEO role, the company faced various challenges. However, in 2007, Dell returned as CEO, leading a successful turnaround effort to reinvigorate the company's growth and competitiveness.

Beyond his role at Dell, Michael Dell is known for his philanthropic efforts. In 1999, he and his wife, Susan, established the Michael & Susan Dell Foundation, a charitable organization focused on improving educational opportunities, children's health, and economic stability for underserved communities. The foundation has made significant contributions to various educational initiatives and social causes, positively impacting the lives of countless individuals.

Michael Dell's entrepreneurial journey exemplifies the power of vision, innovation, and adaptability. His disruptive approach to the computer industry, coupled with his unwavering commitment to customer satisfaction, has reshaped the way technology is manufactured, sold, and experienced. Dell Inc.'s success serves as a testament to the transformative impact of a customer-centric business model.

As we delve into the remarkable story of Michael Dell, we witness his remarkable ability to anticipate market trends, adapt to changing landscapes, and foster a culture of innovation within his company. His legacy as a visionary entrepreneur continues to inspire aspiring business leaders to challenge the status quo, embrace technology's potential, and prioritize the needs of their customers.

Michael Dell's relentless pursuit of excellence and his dedication to making a positive impact in the world have cemented his position as a respected figure in the technology industry and beyond. His entrepreneurial journey serves as a testament to the transformative power of bold ideas, strategic vision, and unwavering determination.

41. Robin Li

As the co-founder and CEO of Baidu, Robin Li has made significant contributions to the evolution of the internet and search technology, transforming the way people access information in China and beyond.

Born in 1968 in Yangquan, Shanxi province, China, Robin Li showed a passion for computer science and mathematics from an early age. After completing his undergraduate studies at Peking University, he pursued a Ph.D. in computer science at the State University of New York at Buffalo. It was during this time that Li developed an interest in search engines and the potential they held for organizing and accessing vast amounts of online information.

In 2000, along with Eric Xu, Robin Li co-founded Baidu, initially as a search engine for Chinese websites. Li's vision was to provide Chinese internet users with a search engine that understood their language, culture, and specific needs. Baidu quickly gained popularity, offering Chinese-language search results and tailored services to cater to the unique characteristics of the Chinese market.

Under Robin Li's leadership, Baidu experienced rapid growth and became the dominant search engine in China. Li's deep understanding of the Chinese market and his focus on providing relevant and reliable search results played a pivotal role in Baidu's success. He implemented algorithms and technologies to improve search accuracy and relevance, enabling users to find information quickly and efficiently.

Li's entrepreneurial vision extended beyond search. He diversified Baidu's offerings by introducing new products and services, including Baidu Maps, Baidu Baike (an online encyclopedia), Baidu Wallet (a mobile payment platform), and Baidu Cloud (cloud storage services). This diversification strategy expanded Baidu's influence and solidified its position as a comprehensive internet services provider.

Recognizing the growing importance of artificial intelligence (AI) and machine learning, Robin Li has been instrumental in transforming Baidu into an AI-centric company. Baidu's Apollo project, an open-source platform for autonomous driving, and its AI research institute, Baidu Research, have showcased the company's commitment to driving innovation and pushing the boundaries of technology.

Robin Li's entrepreneurial achievements have not gone unnoticed. He has received numerous accolades and recognition for his contributions to the technology industry. Li's leadership and entrepreneurial spirit have inspired a new generation of Chinese entrepreneurs, fueling a culture of innovation and technological advancement.

Beyond his role at Baidu, Robin Li is involved in philanthropic initiatives focused on education, environmental conservation, and disaster relief efforts. His commitment to social responsibility has earned him admiration and respect, further solidifying his influence and impact.

Robin Li's entrepreneurial journey exemplifies the transformative power of search technology and the potential for innovation in the digital age. His unwavering commitment to providing relevant and reliable search results, his focus on the Chinese market, and his exploration of emerging technologies have shaped the internet landscape in China and influenced global search trends.

As we explore the remarkable story of Robin Li, we witness his visionary leadership, determination, and ability to anticipate and adapt to market trends. His entrepreneurial journey serves as an inspiration to aspiring business leaders, highlighting the importance of understanding one's audience, leveraging technology, and driving innovation to create meaningful and transformative products and services.

42. Zhang Yiming

Zhang Yiming: a name that has become synonymous with viral videos, short-form content, and the global sensation known as TikTok. As the founder and former CEO of ByteDance, Zhang Yiming has made a profound impact on the world of social media and entertainment, reshaping how we consume and engage with online content.

Born in 1983 in Longyan, Fujian province, China, Zhang Yiming demonstrated an early fascination with technology and programming. After earning a bachelor's degree in Software Engineering from Nankai University, Zhang embarked on his entrepreneurial journey, founding several ventures before establishing ByteDance in 2012.

Initially focused on developing news aggregation platforms, Zhang Yiming saw the potential of short-form video content and launched Douyin in China in 2016. Douyin quickly gained traction, captivating users with its addictive and easily digestible videos. Recognizing the international appeal of the platform, Zhang expanded globally and rebranded Douyin as TikTok, which became a worldwide phenomenon, reaching billions of users and dominating the social media landscape.

Zhang's genius lies in his ability to understand user behavior and preferences, leveraging algorithms and artificial intelligence to deliver personalized content recommendations. TikTok's addictive nature, combined with its seamless user experience and powerful algorithm, propelled it to unprecedented heights of popularity, particularly among younger demographics.

Under Zhang Yiming's leadership, ByteDance diversified its offerings beyond TikTok. The company acquired Musical.ly, a popular lip-syncing app, and merged it with TikTok to further expand its reach. Additionally, Zhang oversaw the development of other successful apps, including Toutiao (a news aggregation platform), Xigua Video (a short video app), and Helo (a social networking platform). ByteDance's portfolio of apps collectively reaches billions of users worldwide.

Zhang's entrepreneurial success has not come without challenges. ByteDance faced scrutiny over content moderation and privacy concerns, particularly in relation to TikTok's operations in certain countries. However, Zhang remained committed to addressing these issues, implementing stricter content policies and transparency measures to ensure a safe and positive user experience.

Zhang Yiming's entrepreneurial journey exemplifies the transformative power of social media and the impact of personalized content in today's digital age. His ability to anticipate trends, adapt to user preferences, and harness the potential of AI-driven algorithms has revolutionized the way we consume and create online content.

Beyond his accomplishments in the tech industry, Zhang is known for his humility, quiet demeanor, and focus on work-life balance. He has expressed a desire to maintain a low profile and has placed importance on the well-being and development of his employees. His leadership style and commitment to fostering a positive work culture have contributed to ByteDance's success and employee satisfaction.

As we explore the remarkable story of Zhang Yiming, we witness his entrepreneurial spirit, innovative mindset, and his unwavering commitment to pushing the boundaries of social media and technology. His journey serves as an inspiration to aspiring entrepreneurs, highlighting the importance of understanding user needs, embracing emerging technologies, and staying ahead of the curve to create groundbreaking products and platforms that captivate audiences worldwide.

43. Jay Chaudhry

Jay Chaudhry: a name synonymous with cybersecurity innovation, visionary leadership, and the transformation of how organizations approach cloud security. As the founder and CEO of Zscaler, Jay Chaudhry has played a pivotal role in revolutionizing the way businesses protect their digital assets in the era of cloud computing.

Born and raised in India, Jay Chaudhry developed a passion for technology and computer science from a young age. He embarked on an academic journey, earning a bachelor's degree in Mathematics and Physics from the Birla Institute of Technology and Science (BITS) in Pilani, India, and later obtaining a master's degree in Electrical Engineering from the University of Cincinnati, USA.

Chaudhry's entrepreneurial journey began when he co-founded AirDefense, a wireless security company that pioneered the concept of securing Wi-Fi networks. This venture showcased his deep understanding of the security landscape and his ability to identify emerging threats in the digital realm.

In 2007, Jay Chaudhry founded Zscaler, a cloud-based security company that provides organizations with a unified platform to secure their networks and protect against cyber threats. Recognizing the rapid adoption of cloud computing and the challenges it presented in terms of traditional perimeter-based security models,

Chaudhry developed a visionary approach known as Zero Trust Security.

Zscaler's Zero Trust Security model operates on the principle that no user or device should be automatically trusted, regardless of their location or network. By routing internet traffic through its cloud platform, Zscaler inspects and filters data in real-time, providing organizations with comprehensive security controls and visibility across their network, regardless of the user's location or device.

Under Jay Chaudhry's leadership, Zscaler has experienced significant growth and has become a leader in the cloud security industry. The company's innovative approach has garnered recognition from customers, analysts, and industry experts alike. Zscaler's solutions enable organizations to embrace the benefits of cloud computing while ensuring their digital assets and sensitive data remain secure.

Chaudhry's impact extends beyond Zscaler. He is an advocate for cybersecurity awareness and has been actively involved in industry initiatives to improve security practices and address evolving threats. His thought leadership and expertise in the field have led to speaking engagements at major conferences and universities, where he shares his insights and perspectives on cybersecurity.

Jay Chaudhry's entrepreneurial journey is characterized by his ability to anticipate market trends, identify gaps in security strategies, and develop innovative solutions that address emerging challenges. His vision for Zero Trust Security has reshaped the cybersecurity landscape, challenging traditional notions of perimeter-based protection and highlighting the importance of continuous monitoring and protection in the cloud era.

Beyond his professional accomplishments, Jay Chaudhry is known for his philanthropic efforts. He and his wife, Renu Chaudhry, established the Chaudhry Family Foundation, which supports education and healthcare initiatives in underserved communities around the world.

As we explore the remarkable story of Jay Chaudhry, we witness his entrepreneurial spirit, commitment to innovation, and dedication to making the digital world a safer place. His journey serves as an inspiration to aspiring entrepreneurs and cybersecurity professionals, emphasizing the importance of thinking beyond traditional security approaches and embracing new paradigms to protect against evolving threats in our increasingly connected world.

44. Patrick Collison

As the co-founder and CEO of Stripe, Patrick Collinson has played a pivotal role in reshaping the landscape of digital commerce and enabling businesses of all sizes to easily accept online payments.

Born and raised in Ireland, Patrick Collinson's entrepreneurial journey began at an early age. While studying physics at the Massachusetts Institute of Technology (MIT), he and his brother, John Collinson, founded Auctomatic, a software company that helped manage and streamline the auction process online. This early venture provided a glimpse into the vast potential of the internet and the challenges faced by businesses in accepting online payments.

In 2010, Patrick Collinson, along with his brother John, launched Stripe, a revolutionary online payment processing platform. The vision behind Stripe was to simplify the complexities of accepting online payments and provide businesses with a seamless and developer-friendly solution. By offering a unified API and easy integration capabilities, Stripe empowered businesses to accept payments from customers around the world, regardless of their location or preferred payment method.

Stripe's success can be attributed to Collinson's relentless focus on the customer experience and his commitment to delivering innovative solutions. Through continuous iteration and improvement, Stripe has expanded its services to include features such as fraud prevention, subscription management, and invoicing, offering businesses a comprehensive suite of tools to manage their online transactions.

Under Patrick Collinson's leadership, Stripe has experienced exponential growth and garnered recognition as one of the most valuable and influential fintech companies in the world. Its client roster includes some of the biggest names in the tech industry, e-commerce, and the gig economy. By providing businesses with the infrastructure and tools to seamlessly accept payments, Stripe has fueled the growth of online businesses and helped democratize access to the global digital marketplace.

Collinson's entrepreneurial success extends beyond Stripe. He is known for his strategic investments and support of emerging startups, particularly in the fintech and technology sectors. His expertise and insights are highly sought after, and he has been a speaker at major industry conferences and events, sharing his experiences and perspectives on the future of digital payments and e-commerce.

Patrick Collinson's entrepreneurial journey exemplifies the transformative power of simplifying complex processes and providing innovative solutions to enable businesses to thrive in the digital age. His relentless pursuit of customer-centricity, focus on technological advancements, and commitment to excellence have redefined the online payments landscape and set new standards for the industry.

Beyond his professional achievements, Collinson is actively involved in philanthropy and has supported various charitable initiatives. His commitment to making a positive impact extends to initiatives focused on education, healthcare, and economic empowerment.

As we explore the remarkable story of Patrick Collinson, we

witness his entrepreneurial spirit, vision, and dedication to revolutionizing the world of online payments. His journey serves as an inspiration to aspiring entrepreneurs, highlighting the importance of identifying and addressing market needs, fostering innovation, and empowering businesses to succeed in the ever-evolving digital ecosystem.

45. John Zimmer

As the co-founder and president of Lyft, John Zimmer has played a pivotal role in revolutionizing the ride-sharing industry and reshaping how people commute in cities around the world.

Born and raised in the United States, John Zimmer demonstrated an early passion for entrepreneurship and a keen interest in the intersection of technology and transportation. After completing his studies at Cornell University's School of Hotel Administration, Zimmer delved into the world of real estate and gained valuable insights into the challenges faced by commuters and urban dwellers.

In 2012, John Zimmer co-founded Lyft, a peer-to-peer ride-sharing platform that connects passengers with drivers through a mobile app. Lyft's mission was to create a more efficient, affordable, and sustainable transportation system that would reduce congestion and provide an alternative to traditional taxi services.

Zimmer's vision for Lyft went beyond mere convenience. He believed that ride-sharing had the potential to build a sense of community, foster human connections, and create economic opportunities for drivers. Lyft's emphasis on friendly, personable drivers and the ability for passengers to sit in the front seat were intentional choices that aimed to create a more welcoming and inclusive experience.

Under Zimmer's leadership, Lyft grew rapidly, expanding its services to major cities across the United States and eventually branching out internationally. The company's user-friendly app, competitive pricing, and focus on safety and customer satisfaction resonated with millions of users, positioning Lyft as one of the leading ride-sharing platforms in the world.

Beyond ride-sharing, John Zimmer has been a vocal advocate for the advancement of autonomous vehicles. He envisions a future where self-driving cars will not only enhance the efficiency and safety of transportation but also transform cities by reducing the need for private car ownership and freeing up valuable urban space.

Zimmer's entrepreneurial success extends beyond Lyft. He is actively involved in industry initiatives and has been a speaker at conferences, sharing his insights on the future of transportation and the potential impact of emerging technologies. Zimmer's innovative thinking, strategic mindset, and passion for creating positive change have earned him recognition as a prominent figure in the transportation industry.

As an entrepreneur, John Zimmer embodies the spirit of disruption and innovation. His vision for Lyft, combined with his unwavering commitment to providing reliable, affordable, and sustainable transportation options, has reshaped the way people commute and has had a profound impact on urban mobility.

Beyond his professional endeavors, Zimmer is involved in philanthropy and social initiatives. He has supported causes related to education, social justice, and community development, further demonstrating his commitment to making a positive impact in the world.

As we explore the remarkable story of John Zimmer, we witness his entrepreneurial spirit, dedication to improving transportation, and commitment to building a more connected and sustainable future. His journey serves as an inspiration to aspiring entrepreneurs, highlighting the importance of addressing societal challenges, embracing innovation, and leveraging technology to create positive change in our communities and beyond.

46. Logan Green

As the co-founder and CEO of Lyft, Logan Green has played a pivotal role in revolutionizing the way people move around cities and reimagining the future of urban transportation.

Logan Green's passion for transportation and sustainability emerged from his early experiences and observations while growing up in Southern California. Witnessing the challenges of congestion, pollution, and limited access to efficient transportation options, Green became determined to find a solution that would not only alleviate these issues but also create a more connected and sustainable world.

In 2007, Logan Green co-founded Zimride, a long-distance ridesharing platform that aimed to optimize vehicle occupancy and reduce the number of cars on the road. Recognizing the potential to extend this concept to urban environments, Green and his co-founder, John Zimmer, launched Lyft in 2012, transforming Zimride into a peer-to-peer ridesharing service accessible to anyone with a smartphone.

Lyft's mission was clear: to create a more efficient, affordable, and sustainable transportation system by connecting riders with drivers through a user-friendly mobile app. The platform empowered individuals to become drivers and earn income while providing convenient and reliable transportation options to passengers.

Under Logan Green's leadership, Lyft grew rapidly, expanding its services across the United States and eventually reaching global markets. The company's emphasis on community, safety, and customer satisfaction set it apart from traditional transportation providers. Lyft's signature pink mustache and the friendly, personable nature of its drivers created a unique and welcoming experience that resonated with millions of users.

Beyond ride-sharing, Logan Green has been a staunch advocate for the future of autonomous vehicles. He envisions a world where self-driving cars will not only enhance safety and convenience but also reduce traffic congestion and environmental impact. Lyft has actively pursued partnerships and collaborations with leading technology and automotive companies to accelerate the development and deployment of autonomous vehicles.

Green's entrepreneurial journey extends beyond Lyft. He is actively involved in initiatives that promote sustainability, urban planning, and transportation policy. His thought leadership and expertise in the field have led to speaking engagements at major conferences and universities, where he shares his insights and perspectives on the future of transportation.

As an entrepreneur, Logan Green embodies the spirit of innovation and social impact. His vision for Lyft, combined with his dedication to creating a more connected and sustainable world, has transformed the way people think about transportation and has had a profound impact on urban mobility.

Beyond his professional accomplishments, Green is committed to philanthropy and social initiatives. He has supported causes related to education, sustainability, and access to transportation, exemplifying his belief in using technology and entrepreneurship to create positive change.

As we delve into the remarkable story of Logan Green, we witness his entrepreneurial drive, commitment to sustainable transportation, and relentless pursuit of a future where mobility is accessible and environmentally conscious. His journey serves as an inspiration to aspiring entrepreneurs, highlighting the power of innovation, collaboration, and a shared vision to transform industries and improve the lives of people around the world.

47. Kevin Ryan

As a pioneering entrepreneur and visionary leader, Kevin Ryan has left an indelible mark on the tech industry and has played a significant role in shaping the digital landscape.

Hailing from the United States, Kevin Ryan embarked on his entrepreneurial journey with an impressive educational background. He earned his Bachelor's degree from Yale University and went on to obtain an MBA from INSEAD. Equipped with a strong academic foundation and a drive for success, Ryan ventured into the world of business with a determination to make a difference.

Ryan's journey took off during the early days of the dot-com boom. He co-founded DoubleClick in 1996, a groundbreaking online advertising platform that helped revolutionize digital marketing. Under Ryan's leadership as the CEO, DoubleClick grew into a dominant force in the industry, providing innovative solutions to advertisers and publishers and playing a pivotal role in shaping the online advertising landscape.

After the successful acquisition of DoubleClick by Google, Kevin Ryan continued to make his mark as a serial entrepreneur and investor. He co-founded numerous ventures, each with a unique focus and the potential for disruptive impact. Some notable companies he helped establish include Gilt Groupe, a luxury e-commerce platform; Business Insider, a leading digital media publication; and MongoDB, a popular open-source database software provider.

Throughout his entrepreneurial journey, Kevin Ryan has demonstrated a keen eye for identifying emerging trends and leveraging them to create successful businesses. He has a knack for assembling talented teams, fostering innovation, and executing strategic plans. His ability to anticipate market needs and adapt to changing dynamics has allowed him to stay ahead of the curve and consistently deliver value.

In addition to his entrepreneurial pursuits, Kevin Ryan has been actively involved in fostering the growth and development of the tech ecosystem. He has served as a mentor, advisor, and investor for numerous startups, providing guidance and support to budding entrepreneurs. His insights and expertise are highly sought after, and he has been recognized as a thought leader in the industry.

Beyond his professional accomplishments, Kevin Ryan is committed to philanthropy and social impact. He has dedicated his time and resources to initiatives focused on education, healthcare, and community development. His belief in using technology and entrepreneurship to drive positive change is evident in his commitment to making a difference in society.

As we explore the remarkable story of Kevin Ryan, we witness his entrepreneurial spirit, strategic mindset, and commitment to innovation. His journey serves as an inspiration to aspiring entrepreneurs, highlighting the importance of seizing opportunities, embracing disruption, and continually pushing boundaries to create meaningful impact in the business world and beyond.

48. Jack Ma

Jack Ma, born Ma Yun on September 10, 1964, in Hangzhou, China, is a renowned entrepreneur, philanthropist, and former executive chairman of Alibaba Group, one of the world's largest e-commerce conglomerates. His story is a testament to perseverance, resilience, and the transformative power of embracing opportunities in the face of adversity.

Ma's journey began with humble beginnings. Raised in a modest family, he faced numerous challenges throughout his early life. Despite these obstacles, Ma developed a passion for learning and a deep curiosity about the world. As a young student, he displayed a keen interest in English and spent time practicing his language skills by conversing with foreign tourists in his hometown.

Ma's entrepreneurial spirit emerged during his college years. After facing rejections from various job applications, including a now-famous rejection from KFC, he persevered and eventually found work as an English teacher at Hangzhou Dianzi University. It was during this time that Ma's encounter with the internet sparked a new vision within him.

In 1995, Ma traveled to the United States as part of a government-sponsored trip, where he was first exposed to the internet. Recognizing the vast potential of this emerging technology, he became determined to bring the internet revolution to China. Upon returning to China, Ma founded China Yellow Pages, an online directory that aimed to connect Chinese businesses with customers around the world.

In 1999, Ma, along with a group of co-founders, established Alibaba, an online marketplace that aimed to revolutionize e-commerce in China. Starting with a small team operating out of his apartment, Ma's vision was to create a platform that would empower small and medium-sized enterprises (SMEs) to thrive in the digital age.

Alibaba faced numerous challenges in its early years, including skepticism from investors and a highly competitive market. However, Ma's unwavering belief in the potential of the internet and his relentless pursuit of innovation allowed Alibaba to overcome these obstacles. The company launched its flagship platform, Alibaba.com, which connected Chinese suppliers with global buyers, and quickly became a leading player in the e-commerce industry.

Under Ma's leadership, Alibaba expanded its services to include Taobao, a consumer-to-consumer online marketplace, and Tmall, a business-to-consumer platform. These platforms transformed the way people in China and around the world bought and sold goods, propelling Alibaba to unparalleled success.

In 2014, Alibaba made history with its initial public offering (IPO) on the New York Stock Exchange, raising a record-breaking amount of capital and becoming one of the world's most valuable technology companies. Ma's vision and entrepreneurial spirit had transformed Alibaba into a global powerhouse, revolutionizing e-commerce and reshaping the digital landscape.

Throughout his career, Ma has been a champion of entrepreneurship and a vocal advocate for empowering small businesses. He has inspired countless individuals with his philosophy of embracing failure, taking risks, and embracing change. Ma's leadership and vision have also extended beyond Alibaba, as he has been actively involved in philanthropy, focusing on education, environmental sustainability, and healthcare.

In 2019, Ma stepped down as executive chairman of Alibaba, choosing to focus on his philanthropic endeavors and other passions. His impact on the business world and society at large continues to be felt, and his story serves as an inspiration to aspiring entrepreneurs and leaders worldwide.

Jack Ma's journey exemplifies the transformative power of perseverance, seizing opportunities, and believing in one's vision. From humble beginnings to revolutionizing e-commerce and advocating for small businesses, his story serves as a reminder that with determination and a bold entrepreneurial spirit, one can overcome obstacles and shape the future.

49. Payal Kadakia

As the co-founder and former CEO of ClassPass, Payal Kadakia has made a significant impact on the fitness industry and has empowered individuals to discover and engage in a wide range of fitness activities.

Born and raised in the United States, Payal Kadakia's journey began with a deep passion for dance. As a trained dancer herself, she recognized the challenges faced by individuals who sought to participate in different fitness classes and activities. Kadakia envisioned a solution that would simplify the process of finding and booking fitness classes, providing people with greater access to a variety of workout options.

In 2011, Kadakia co-founded ClassPass, a groundbreaking fitness platform that offers users the flexibility to choose from a diverse selection of fitness classes at various studios and gyms. With a user-friendly app and a subscription-based model, ClassPass revolutionized the fitness industry by giving users the freedom to explore different workout styles and venues without being tied to a single gym membership.

Under Payal Kadakia's leadership, ClassPass experienced exponential growth, expanding its services to major cities around the world. The platform's innovative approach to fitness gained popularity, attracting both fitness enthusiasts and those seeking to incorporate physical activity into their daily lives. By providing access to a wide range of fitness classes, from yoga and pilates to spinning and boxing, ClassPass empowered individuals to personalize their fitness journey and discover new ways to stay active.

Kadakia's entrepreneurial success extends beyond ClassPass. She is a vocal advocate for women's empowerment and diversity in the tech industry. Recognizing the underrepresentation of women in leadership roles, Kadakia co-founded the "The Sa Dance Company" and launched the "Chaat Shop" to celebrate and promote Indian culture. She has also been involved in mentorship programs and initiatives aimed at supporting and inspiring aspiring entrepreneurs, particularly women, to pursue their dreams.

Payal Kadakia's entrepreneurial journey exemplifies the power of passion, determination, and innovation. Her vision for ClassPass, combined with her unwavering commitment to promoting physical fitness and well-being, has transformed the way people approach their fitness routines and has had a positive impact on the fitness industry as a whole.

Beyond her professional achievements, Kadakia is actively involved in philanthropy and social initiatives. She has supported causes related to education, healthcare, and women's empowerment, further demonstrating her commitment to making a positive impact in society.

As we delve into the remarkable story of Payal Kadakia, we witness her entrepreneurial spirit, dedication to promoting fitness and well-being, and commitment to empowering individuals through technology. Her journey serves as an inspiration to aspiring entrepreneurs, highlighting the importance of pursuing one's passions, embracing innovation, and leveraging technology to create positive change in the lives of others.

50. Anne Wojcicki

As the co-founder and CEO of 23andMe, Anne Wojcicki has played a crucial role in revolutionizing the way individuals access and understand their genetic information, empowering them to make informed decisions about their health and well-being.

Born and raised in the United States, Anne Wojcicki's passion for healthcare and genetics was deeply influenced by her academic background. She graduated with a degree in Biology from Yale University and went on to pursue a career in healthcare investing. It was during this time that Wojcicki recognized the need to make genetic information more accessible and understandable to the general public.

In 2006, Anne Wojcicki co-founded 23andMe, a direct-to-consumer genetic testing company. The company's mission was to empower individuals with knowledge about their own DNA, allowing them to gain insights into their ancestry, genetic traits, and potential health risks. 23andMe's user-friendly DNA testing kits and interactive online platform made it possible for individuals to explore their genetic makeup from the comfort of their own homes.

Under Wojcicki's leadership, 23andMe grew rapidly, attracting millions of users who were eager to uncover their genetic information and learn more about their health. The company's personalized reports provided users with valuable insights into their genetic predispositions, enabling them to make informed decisions about their lifestyle choices, healthcare, and family planning.

Beyond genetic testing, Anne Wojcicki has been a vocal advocate for personalized healthcare and the importance of data-driven medicine. She has championed the use of big data and genetic research to advance scientific discoveries and improve healthcare outcomes. By aggregating and analyzing anonymized genetic data from consenting individuals, 23andMe has contributed to groundbreaking research in areas such as genetic diseases, drug development, and population health.

Wojcicki's entrepreneurial success extends beyond 23andMe. She has been actively involved in various initiatives aimed at promoting scientific research, genetic literacy, and healthcare access. Her advocacy for patient rights and data privacy has played a pivotal role in shaping the regulatory landscape for direct-to-consumer genetic testing.

Anne Wojcicki's entrepreneurial journey exemplifies the power of democratizing healthcare and enabling individuals to take charge of their own health. Her vision for 23andMe, combined with her commitment to leveraging genetic data for scientific advancements, has transformed the way people perceive and engage with their genetic information.

Beyond her professional accomplishments, Wojcicki is actively involved in philanthropy and social initiatives. She has supported causes related to education, scientific research, and women's empowerment, further demonstrating her commitment to making a positive impact in society.

As we explore the remarkable story of Anne Wojcicki, we witness her entrepreneurial spirit, dedication to personalized healthcare, and advocacy for genetic literacy. Her journey serves as an inspiration to aspiring entrepreneurs, highlighting the importance of leveraging technology and data to drive innovation and improve the lives of individuals worldwide.

About the Author

Daniel Boyd is an accomplished business strategist, thought leader, and author specializing in guiding business leaders towards innovative and effective decision-making. With over two decades of experience in the corporate world, Daniel has honed his expertise in various industries, ranging from technology to finance and beyond. He is known for his deep understanding of business dynamics and his ability to distill complex concepts into practical frameworks that drive organizational success.

Daniel's passion for empowering business leaders to think critically and strategically has led him to write a range of books in the business niche. Drawing on his extensive experience and research, Daniel presents a comprehensive collection of frameworks and concepts that equip leaders with the tools they need to navigate the complexities of the business landscape.

When he is not immersed in the world of business, Daniel enjoys spending time with his family, exploring new cultures through travel, and indulging in outdoor activities that rejuvenate his mind and inspire his creativity.

Other Titles You Might Enjoy:

The Empowered Entrepreneurs Series
50 Founders Stories
50 Innovative Companies
20 Ways to Use AI In Your Small Business

Income Builders Series
Start With $0: Unleashing the Power of Internet Money
50 Side Hustle Ideas for Australians
Make Money Grow on Trees

A Business Leaders Guide To
50 IT Concepts for Business Leaders
50 Operations Concepts for Business Leaders
50 Legal Concepts for Business Leaders
50 Economics Concepts for Business Leaders
50 Finance Concepts for Business Leaders
50 HR Concepts for Business Leaders
50 Management Concepts for Business Leaders
50 Marketing Concepts for Business Leaders
50 Sales Concepts for Business Leaders
50 ESG Concepts for Business Leaders
100 Frameworks & Concepts for Business Leaders

The CEO's Playbook Series

The Diversity, Equity & Inclusion Playbook
The Recession Playbook
The Branding & Reputation Playbook
The Artificial Intelligence Playbook
The Future of Work Playbook
The Web3, Metaverse and Virtual Reality Playbook
The Mastering Client Engagement Playbook
The Cybersecurity and Cybercrime Playbook
The Climate Crisis Playbook
The 21st Economy Playbook

147